farmer's market cooking

farmer's market cooking

A Complete Guide to Selecting and Preparing the Freshest Foods for All Seasons

Sally Ann Berk

Photographs by Zeva Oelbaum

Paperbacks

Published by
Black Dog & Leventhal Publishers, Inc.
151 West 19th Street
New York, NY 10011

Distributed by
Workman Publishing Company
708 Broadway
New York, NY 10003

Manufactured in The United Kingdom

Library of Congress Cataloging-i-Publication Data

Berk, Sally Ann.
[Farmer's market guide and cookbook]
Farmer's market cooking: a complete guide to selecting & preparing the
freshest food for all seasons / by Sally Ann Berk.

p.cm.
Originally published: Farmer's market guide and cook book. 1996
ISBN 1-57912-173-X (pbk.)
1. Cookery, American. 2.Farm produce. I. Title

TX715 .B4829 2001
641.5973--dc2 2001018416

ISBN: 1-57912-173-X

h g f e d c b a

Many thanks to the following people whose advice, knowledge, and help
was invaluable: Daniel H. Berk of Nature's Fresh Northwest; Ted Snyder of
the Portland Farmers' Market and Morning Star Farms; Will Davis, Kiwi
grower, of Gridley, California; Michael and Sally Hiebert of Northwest
Connection; Managers and vendors of the Oakland Farmers' Market at Jack
London Square; Helen Johnson of the Massachusetts Department of
Agriculture; Irene Wood of the Tanana Valley Farmer's Market;
Denny N. Johnson of the United States Department of Agriculture; Everyone
on CompuServe and the Net who gave me virtual tours of their local
markets; Special thanks to Nicole Reisman and Joe Antonishek for their
delicious recipes; and James G. Wakeman.

This book was originally published under the title
The Farmer's Market Guide and Cookbook

Cover design by 27.12 design, Ltd., NYC

Contents

Introduction

Many of us have lost the sense of where we are in the world, our connection to it and to each other. We buy our milk in plastic jugs at the corner store, we load up on fruits and vegetables at the supermarket without giving a second thought to where they came from or how they were grown, we feed ourselves and our children over-processed foods loaded with unnecessary and often harmful ingredients. We are quickly becoming an alienated society with an ever-decreasing sense of community—and that is something that we need. As we grow closer to becoming just another bit of code on a microchip, it is important that we reinvent the idea of community. One of the small but good and true ways to start doing this is to buy your food at your local farmers' market.

If there is a market in your neighborhood, you may have been thinking about going but haven't yet got around to it. Or you may not know if you have one where you live, but would like to find out. You might even feel a little intimidated shopping directly from the farmers at their stands.

This book will guide you through (or to) your local farmers' market and show you how to avail yourself of the wonderful things you'll find there. It will tell you how to choose your produce and when to start looking for seasonal fruits and vegetables—the first juicy peach of summer, the first tender spring asparagus. It will give you questions to ask the growers about what they do, and introduce you to some of the people who are the farmers' markets.

WHERE TO START

Look in our directory to see which market is closest to you. If you don't find one near your home, call your city hall, chamber of commerce or county cooperative extension. There are new Farmers' Markets and community markets popping up every week, so some may not appear in this book.

Once you've found your market, go! Put a cooler in your trunk. Bring a big cloth tote bag and lots of small bills and pocket change—growers hate to break twenties. Keep your money in your front pocket. Markets can get very busy and transactions are much easier if you are not fumbling around for your wallet. Wear comfortable shoes and a hat if you're going to an outdoor market.

WHAT TO DO

When you get there, first stroll around and take in all of the sites—see what's there. Grab some coffee and a freshly baked cinnamon roll from one of the bakers at the market and enjoy the atmosphere for a while. Then you are ready to shop!

Lots of produce looks good, and the individual entries in this book will tell you how to choose well, but the true test is taste. Any grower worth her salt will let you taste before you buy. Try as many peaches as you can before you decide which you will buy. Lemon curd is expensive, so ask for a sample before you invest. It is not an imposition to do so—people who make the condiments or cheese, or grow the apples are delighted to let you taste them. (Just try that at a supermarket!)

Until you become accustomed to shopping at the market, it will be all-to-easy to buy everything in sight. Everything looks so good, smells great, and tastes divine, but unless you're canning, five pounds of peaches for one person will be wasteful. And can you really eat two sourdough baguettes in two days? It helps to take a shopping list. Try to stick to it if you can. It's hard: Those organic strawberries look so good. . . can I just taste one . . ?

If you want to buy fruit or vegetables in bulk for canning or anyother reason, talk to the grower. She will almost always strike a deal with you if you buy over a certain quantity.

WHAT'S THERE

Markets vary from season to season and place to place, but they all have produce. Many markets are branching out in gourmet directions, and hosting vendors who sell all kinds of food products. You will find baked goods, organic meats and free-range fowl, nitrate-free sausages, condiments, honey, fresh and smoked fish, cheeses and milk, eggs, fresh pasta, and sauces. Sometimes local wineries sell their varietals and offer tastings. Almost any food you buy at the supermarket will be available at the farmers' market, but it will be fresher and almost always cheaper. Many people have made the market such a habit that they only go to the supermarket for paper goods.

WHAT'S ORGANIC

Organic produce and other organic foods are always available at farmers' markets. Some markets are organic only. But organic may cost more. Should you buy it?

Really, it's your choice. If you peel everything before you eat it, or wash it well, then conventionally grown food is probably OK. But, besides tasting better, organic produce is cleaner and safer for you and your kids. There are many pesticides being used that are approved by the FDA but can have harrowing cumulative effects on children and adults. Cancer among farmers who use pesticides is statistically higher than for many other occupations. Meat and fowl raised with antibiotics is downright dangerous and should be avoided.

Check with your local market manager to find out what constitutes "organic" in your state or province. The definition varies from state to state. Look for official organic certification, from either the state or a recognized certification group. Just because a sign says something is organic doesn't mean it's true.

But remember, organic farmers are the stewards of the land. Their soil is healthier and richer in minerals than chemically blanched soil. They produce less waste, because much is recycled, and there is no chemical runoff into the water table.

WHAT DO I DO WITH IT

You've just bought some chard. It was gorgeous, green and leafy—you had to have it. But you've never prepared chard. What do you do with it? Talk to the grower. She will give you preparation tips and maybe even some recipes. Some growers and vendors give out recipe cards with their products. Learn from the experts. They usually know what they're doing. Or, flip to tomatoes in this book and see what preparation methods are suggested.

IS IT FRESH? IS IT LOCAL?

Take the taste test before buying, as mentioned above—but if you see a tomato in April, that's too early. Don't be afraid to ask how on earth they managed to grow a tomato in early spring. It is unfortunate, but some "growers" merely only go to the major produce wholesalers and then bring imported produce to farmers' markets. Market management is cracking down on this practice, enacting "growers-only" rules, but some people manage to squeak through.

Locally grown produce is always the best. It is the freshest, and you know the most about it. If you see a nectarine in January at the store or the market, it came from South America or New Zealand. Don't buy it. Produce loses flavor as it gets farther from its source. Many of our trade partners are not diligent when it comes to pesticides, so much imported produce has been sprayed with chemicals that have long been banned from use in the United States and Canada.

WHAT NOW?

Enjoy yourself. Eat, drink, talk to the growers and other shoppers. The farmers' market is quickly becoming a weekly gathering for many people. Marriages have been made there (so have divorces), and so have good friends. You will meet your neighbors at the farmers' market, and in this world, that's no small thing.

Ingredients

Note: Each ingredient entry contains from one to four icons indicating the seasonality of that ingredient.

The following is the seasonal icon key:

 Spring

 Summer

 Autumn

 Winter

Major vitamin and mineral content: E, potassium, calcium; good source of dietary fiber

Look for: whole, slivered, raw, blanched, toasted, smoked

Refrigerate: No. Keep in an airtight container.

Freeze: Yes. Freeze in an airtight container if you are not going to use within a few months

Shelf life: 3 to 4 months at room temperature up to a year in the freezer

 Almonds are the kernel of the fruit of the almond tree. They are native to the Mediterranean region, but are now grown in abundance in warmer parts of North America. The almonds you will find at your market are sweet almonds. Because of the high level of potentially lethal prussic acid in bitter almonds, it is illegal to sell them in the United States. Almonds keep well and you should be able to find them all year round. Almonds are great snacks and can be used in just about any type of cooking. Toasting almonds before you use them brings out their flavor and adds crunch to both sweet and savory recipes.

See recipes on pages 170 and 186.

Apples

Major vitamin and mineral content: C, potassium; good source of pectin and dietary fiber

Look for: firm, fragrant fruit; no bruises; bright color

Refrigerate: Yes. Do not wash until ready to eat.

Freeze: No, but canning and preserving are recommended.

Shelf life: 4 to 6 weeks in the refrigerator, depending on variety

Apples (clockwise from top left: Gold, Empire, Green Granny Smith, Stayman Weinsap, Delicious)

Apples are perhaps the most common and popular of all fruits, and because of this, people tend to get blasé about them. That's when the local farmers' market comes in to relieve "apple ennui." The apples in supermarkets have probably been sprayed within an inch of their lives, cold-stored for months, and then shipped hundreds of miles. The apples you'll find at your farmers' market are far superior. You can buy heritage or antique varieties such as Northern Spy, Spitzenberg, and Rhode Island Greening, as well as the better-known Granny Smith, Rome, Delicious, and Jonathan. Some apples, such as Gravensteins, are peculiar to certain parts of the continent. Heritage apples are not grown commercially on a large scale and are rarely shipped, so your farmers' market is probably the only place you'll be able to explore the countless varieties. They are well worth tasting and incorporating into your fruit diet. There are literally hundreds of kinds of apples, each with its own unique qualities. Some are great for baking and cooking, others for eating out of hand or using for juice. Remember that although available year-round in supermarkets, apples are best when they are in season. Apple season is autumn. When you see apples at other times of the year, you know they are not fresh.

See recipes on pages 156, 165 and 200.

Apricots

Major vitamin and mineral content: A, C, E, K, beta carotene, potassium, iron, copper

Look for: fruit that gives just a little when you touch it (not too soft, but not hard); slight bruises are OK; brilliant orange or golden color with a slight pink blush; sweet apricot aroma

Refrigerate: Yes, but ripen at room temperature first.

Freeze: Yes. Slice and freeze in airtight plastic bags or containers.

Shelf life: 1 to 4 days at room temperature

Apricots

Along with peaches and nectarines, fresh, ripe apricots are a sure sign that summer is here. They are tender and sweet. Because they are so fragile, they do not ship well, so your local farmers' market is the best place to look for them. There are several varieties of apricots, from the first-of-the-season Earlicot to the late-season Derby, Blenheim, and Caldwell. Apricots are loaded with vitamins and minerals. If your kids won't eat carrots, give them apricots instead and they'll still be getting the benefits of a food that is high in beta carotene. The versatile apricot makes a great snack and complements many sweet and savory recipes.

See recipe on pages 188.

Artichoke

Major vitamin and mineral content: C, calcium, iron, potassium; good source of dietary fiber

Look for: firm, dense, heavy heads; compact leaves; no withered stems or cracked leaves; some brown spotting is OK

Refrigerate: Yes.

Artichokes

Freeze: No.

Shelf life: 3 to 4 days refrigerated

    Artichokes, the delicious and difficult-to-eat lobster of the vegetable world, are available year-round in artichoke-growing regions. These Italian delicacies, said to have been introduced to France by Catherine de Médicis, are becoming more widely available in the New World. During the spring and winter, artichokes are generally compact, firm, and heavy for their size. In the summer and fall, they tend to be conical in shape and the leaves are not as tightly packed. Artichokes are available in a variety of sizes, from "baby" to jumbo." All are mature when picked, so they are ready to eat when you buy them. Small or baby artichokes weigh about two or three ounces and are ideal for appetizers, casseroles, or sautés. When properly trimmed, every part is edible. Larger artichokes can be steamed and served whole with dips or melted butter, or stuffed for a light meal.

See recipes on pages 129 and 152.

Major vitamin and mineral content: A, C, iron

Look for: fresh, green leaves; no wilting; roots should still be attached

Refrigerate: Yes.

Freeze: No.

Shelf life: 2 days in the refrigerator

   Arugula, also known as rocket, has become an increasingly popular salad green over the past few years and is readily available at most farmers' markets. Its taste is somewhat bitter and peppery, but not unpleasantly so. It is a fine addition to any salad of mixed greens. Arugula is grown outdoors and in greenhouses, so it is usually available. It is extremely perishable, so use it immediately after purchase. It holds much sand and grit, so wash it thoroughly before serving.

See recipe on page 139.

Beans: (clockwise from top left: Black-eyed Beans; Cranberry Beans; Green Lentils; Fava Beans; Adzuki Beans; Garbanzo Beans)

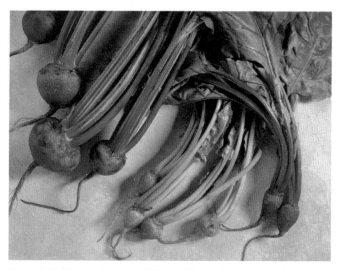

Beets (left: Regular Beets; middle: Golden Baby Beets; right: Baby Beets)

Beets

Major vitamin and mineral content: C, potassium

Look for: fresh, crisp tops; firm beets with smooth skin; smaller beets, which have more flavor

Refrigerate: Yes.

Freeze: No.

Shelf life: greens, 3 to 5 days refrigerated; beets, up to 3 weeks refrigerated

 Beets, red, yellow, and red-and-white-striped, have been a staple of many cultures' diets for thousands of years. The ancient Greeks ate them, and European armies carried them all over the continent and into Asia. Today, beets are ubiquitous and are a nutritious, tasty, and versatile root vegetable. Except for the tough outer skin every part of the beet is edible. If you buy your beets with the greens still attached, be sure to chop them off before refrigerating the beets, because they will leech nutrients from the edible root. Beet greens are wonderful sautéed in oil with garlic or tossed into a salad with other greens. The beet itself is an essential ingredient in borscht and other soups and stews. Pickled beets are great in salads. If you have bad beet memories from childhood, give them another try.

Berries

(blackberries, boysenberries, raspberries, loganberries, marionberries, waldoberries, mulberries, olalliberries, tayberries, black raspberries, thimbleberries)

Major vitamin and mineral content: A, C, calcium, iron, potassium

Look for: plump, undamaged berries with rich color; no mold; no hulls or stems

Refrigerate: Yes. Do not wash until ready to eat.

Freeze: Yes. Spread berries in one layer on a cookie sheet and place in the freezer until completely frozen, then place in an airtight container or plastic bag and freeze for up to a year.

Shelf life: 1 to 2 days in the refrigerator, up to a year in the freezer

The variety of available "drupelet" berries is astonishing. Raspberries are the most common, but at your farmers' market, especially in the summer, you're bound to find exotic and delicious berries that you'll never find at the supermarket. Depending on where you live, you may find all or some of the above-mentioned berries. The same berry may be called by a different name in a different region. A marionberry in

Berries: (clockwise from top left: Tayberries; White Raspberries; Raspberries; Strawberries; Blueberries)

Oregon may be a blackberry in Virginia. A tayberry in Washington State may be a Scottish raspberry in Pennsylvania. The best way to find the berry you like best of all is to taste them. If the farmer will not let you taste one of his berries, go to another stand. Berries are plentiful in season, and you should shop around. Wonderfully tart or amazingly sweet, fresh berries should be eaten right away. You can freeze them to use in recipes later, but they will not maintain their fresh berry consistency.

See recipes on pages 189, 190, and 201.

Major vitamin and mineral content: A, C, potassium

Look for: plump, dry berries; dusty blue color; no green, reddish, moldy, or shriveled berries

Refrigerate: Yes. Do not wash until ready to use.

RAINBOW GARDEN

*L*inda and Larry Addison have been vendors at the Portland Oregon, farmers' market since the day it opened in 1991, and they haven't missed a Saturday since. When their daughter got married, they managed to get their goods to the market and cater her wedding on the same day. You could say these folks have boundless energy, and they do.

Until about five years ago, Larry was a computer executive in the Portland area's growing "silicon forest." After overseeing the successful start-ups of five computer companies, he decided to retire. But Larry and Linda are not "retiring" people. Retirement was simply a way for them to pursue a hobby that had turned into an insatiable habit—cooking and culinary history. They rented a commercial kitchen in Hood River, and Rainbow Garden was born.

Using organic herbs they grow themselves, as well as organic ingredients, including heritage fruits and vegetables mostly purchased from other Portland Farmers' Market vendors, Larry and Linda make a wide range of condiments, pastas, breads, and flours based on recipes in they've found in the antique cookbooks they've collected over the years. Many of their products are based on recipes dating back to the early eighteenth century. They scour cookbooks published in 1930 or earlier for recipes that might appeal to modern palates. After finding a likely candidate, they "translate" the old-fashioned measurements, such as a "glug" of honey, into teaspoons and cups and test the results. The outcome is usually delicious, and many of their friends are happy to be the guinea pigs for potential recipes. Some of the "new" condiments you'll find at their stand include a 1921 blueberry ketchup and a 1739 apple vanilla honey. They are happy to let you taste before you buy. They also produce a line of "zesty sauces," blending fruits, spices, and herbs into marinades and dressings.

The Addisons grind and blend their own flours, which they then use to make their breads, bagels, and tortillas. In addition to their baked goods their flours are also available for purchase at the Market.

And if that weren't enough, Linda and Larry make a line of hand-rolled naturally flavored fettuccini—basil and parsley, sweet red pepper and Parmesan, chile pepper, and lemon and cracked pepper. These pastas are wonderfully flavored and need very little saucing. Other odds and ends at the Rainbow Garden market stand include air-dried organic herbs, oil-free dried tomatoes, a pumpkin pie spice blend with recipe included, pickling spices with suggested recipes, and healthy treats for pets.

In addition to their success at the Market, Linda and Larry have started a mail-order business so you can buy any of their products, as well as gift baskets.

Even if you don't buy a thing from Rainbow Garden at the Portland Farmers' Market, everyone gets a coupon for a free hug.

Linda and Larry Addison
Rainbow Garden
407 June Street
Hood River, OR 97031
503-386-6966
1-800-435-3941

Portland Farmers' Market
1200 NW Front Street, at the Willamette River
Mid-May to mid October
Saturday, 8AM-1PM

Freeze: Yes. Blueberries freeze very well. Spread them in one layer on a cookie sheet and place in the freezer until completely frozen, then put in an airtight container or plastic bag and freeze for up to 1 year.

Shelf life: up to 5 days in the refrigerator, 6 months in the freezer.

Along with raspberries, blueberries could be called the great American summer berry. High-bush or low-bush, these are versatile, flavorful, and almost everyone's favorite. If you live in Maine or eastern Canada, you may be lucky enough to have a grower who sells the wild blueberries and huckleberries that proliferate in August. Tarter than most cultivated berries, these are excellent for jams and preserves.

See recipes on pages 190 and 197.

Bok Choy

Bok choy

Major vitamin and mineral content: A, C, potassium

Look for: crisp, firm, fresh-looking heads; no blemishes; no wilting; leaves should have good, dark green color

Refrigerate: Yes.

Freeze: No.

Shelf life: 2 to 3 days refrigerated

   Bok choy, also known as Chinese white cabbage, is an Asian cousin of Swiss chard and can be used in many of the same ways. Raw or cooked, it is a mild, versatile vegetable that can be used in stir-fries and salads, or alone as a side vegetable. It is becoming increasingly available in most areas of North America.

See recipe on pages 174.

Broccoflower

Major vitamin and mineral content: A, C, calcium, iron, potassium, riboflavin

Look for: firm head; tight florets; bright lime-green color; no black or soft spots

Refrigerate: Yes.

Freeze: Yes. Blanch and store in an airtight container.

Shelf life: up to 1 week refrigerated, 6 months frozen

Broccoflower, also called Romanesco or green cauliflower, is a relative newcomer to the vegetable kingdom. Developed in California in the last ten years, it is a delicious and quite attractive cross between broccoli and cauliflower. Although it has only recently started to appear in farmers' markets outside California, look for it at your market. It combines the best flavor and textural qualities of each parent and can be used in any way you'd prepare broccoli or cauliflower.

Broccoli and Broccoli Rabe

roccoli

Major vitamin and mineral content: A, C, calcium, potassium, riboflavin

Look for: crisp leaves; tightly closed florets; rich green or green with purple color

Refrigerate: Yes.

Freeze: No.

Shelf life: 5 days refrigerated

Broccoli, a relative of cabbage, is a much-loved but often insulted vegetable (think ex-President Bush). It is a true champion in the vegetable kingdom and is loaded with nutrients. To some, broccoli is best served raw, with a yogurt-dill dip. If you want your kids to eat their broccoli, though, you may have to steam it and douse it with a cheese sauce. That's OK. The nutritious value will still shine through. When they grow up, you can introduce them to crudités.

See recipe on pages 169.

it was used primarily for medicinal purposes. Now, it is a ubiquitous and versatile member of our culinary palette. There are two kinds of celery being grown today. You will most likely find the Pascal at your market. This is the celery with which we are all familiar. Always buy it with the leaves on. They are edible and can be added to soups and stocks, or used as garnish. Raw celery is a refreshing crunchy snack, but it can also be cooked into chicken soup and stews.

Chard

Major vitamin and mineral content: A, C, calcium, iron, potassium

Look for: crisp-looking leaves and stalks; no wilting; bright green or green with red color

Refrigerate: Yes.

Red Chard and Green Chard

Freeze: No.

Shelf life: about 3 days refrigerated

Chard, also known as Swiss chard, is a wonderful leafy member of the beet family. It can be found in either the green or red variety. Both are equally nutritious and tasty. It should always be cooked. As we search for more green leafy vegetables to satisfy our needs for the five-a-day fruit and vegetable recommendation, chard has become more popular, and now it can be found at most farmers' markets. Prepare it as you would spinach for a side dish. Try it in soups, or stuff the leaves with other vegetables. The best way to prepare chard, however, may be the simplest. Just clean and chop it, then sauté in a stainless steel pan with olive oil, garlic, nutmeg, and a splash of balsamic vinegar. It is to die for.

See recipe on page 166.

Cherimoya

Major vitamin and mineral content: C, iron, niacin; source of dietary fiber

Look for: dark green scaly skin without blemishes; fruit that's heavy for its size

Refrigerate: Ripen at room temperature until soft, then wrap in paper towels and refrigerate.

Freeze: No.

Shelf life: about 4 days in the refrigerator

This tropical fruit is now being grown in more temperate areas of North America. It is similar to the **Atemoya**, but larger, and its custardy flesh has more of a pineapple-mango flavor. Like the atemoya, it is best chilled, sliced, and eaten with a spoon.

Cherries: (top: Queen Anne Cherries; bottom: Bing Cherries)

Cherries (sweet)

Major vitamin and mineral content: A, C, beta carotene, potassium

Look for: vivid colors; large, shiny, firm fruit with stems still attached

Refrigerate: Yes. Do not wash until ready to eat.

Freeze: Yes. Pit and store in an airtight container.

Shelf life: 2 to 3 days in the refrigerator, up to 6 months in the freezer

Sweet cherries come in many different varieties. Their season is very short, and in most places, you won't able to find any kind of cherry after late July. You will see a much greater variety at your farmers' market than in any supermarket since many of the cherries sold at the farmers' market are very delicate and do not ship well. The first to appear is the Bourlat, a bright red fruit whose season is only about two weeks long. Next come the deep red, almost purple, well-known Bing and the Vans, Lamberts, and Tartarians. These cherries are also found in varying shades of red. Queen Anne and Ranier cherries are yellow with a pink blush. These later sweet cherries may be in season for up to a month. Buy them and eat out of hand. More ambitious folks can pit them (a formidable task) and make wonderful pies and preserves.

Cherries (sour)

Major vitamin and mineral content: A, C, beta carotene, potassium

Look for: small, round, slightly soft fruit

Refrigerate: Yes. Do not wash until ready to use.

Freeze: Pit and freeze in airtight containers.

Shelf life: 1 to 2 days in the refrigerator, 6 months in the freezer

Like its sweet cousin, the sour cherry has a short season. Most sour cherries in North America are processed after harvesting, so fresh ones are difficult to find in a supermarket. But some small farmers do cultivate them, and your best bet for fresh sour cherries is your local farmers' market. Sour cherries are too tart to eat out of hand, but they make wonderful pies and jams, even wine. Some of the varieties you may run into are Early Richmond and Montmorency. They can be yellow, pink, or red.

Chestnuts

Major vitamin and mineral content: potassium

Look for: shells with a deep reddish-brown color; no cracks or blemishes

Refrigerate: Not recommended.

Freeze: No.

Shelf life: 4 to 5 days, stored in a cool, dark, dry place

The chestnut is a cold-weather tradition. Whether you're roaming the canyons of New Mexico or those of midtown Manhattan, the smell of roasting chestnuts is often your companion. These sweet, versatile nuts can also be boiled, preserved, pureed, candied, or used as an ingredient in dressings and savory side dishes. Remove the shells and inner skin and do with them what you will.

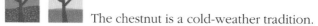

Chile peppers

Major vitamin and mineral content: A, C, potassium

Look for: vivid color; no shriveling or soft spots in fresh chiles; chiles with stems attached

Refrigerate: Yes.

Freeze: Yes. Roast or blanch fresh chiles first and store in airtight containers.

Shelf life: fresh chiles, 3 to 4 days refrigerated; dried chiles, indefinitely

 Fresh chiles

 Dried chiles

Chile peppers, or chiles, can be large or small, deep purplish black or bright green, fiery hot or pleasantly picante. There are more than two hundred varieties of chiles that we know of, and they are all native to the Americas. Generally speaking, the smaller the chile, the more intense the heat. But there are always exceptions to the rules, so be careful when you buy. Ask questions. Some serranos are hotter than others. Some jalapeños are actually not too hot. And even some habaneros (known as the world's hottest pepper) are not as dangerous as their reputation would lead you to believe. Remember when preparing chiles that the heat is concentrated in the membranes and seeds, so remove them if you want less heat. Be careful what you touch—the chile essence will stay on your fingers, so don't rub your eyes (or any other body parts). Some people recommend wearing gloves when working with chiles, but if you're careful, this really isn't necessary. If you want to experiment with chiles, the best place to find the widest variety is, without a doubt, your farmers' market. Chile growers know what they're doing and will tell you exactly what each chile is, how hot it is, and what to do with it. A hint: If your chile recipe turns out too hot for you or your guests, drink some milk. Water only spreads the chile juice around; milk neutralizes it.

See recipes on pages 175 and 184.

Chokecherries

Major vitamin and mineral content: A, C, beta carotene, potassium

Look for: very dark red, small, round, slightly soft fruit

Refrigerate: Yes.

Freeze: Pit and freeze in airtight containers.

Shelf-life: 1 to 2 days in the refrigerator, 6 months in the freezer

Chokecherries are simply wild cherries. They are native to North America and grow almost everywhere. Some small farmers pick them to sell at local farmers' markets. Like sour cherries, they are too tart to eat out of hand, but they make wonderful pies and jams, even wine. Buy them if you see them and start experimenting!

Cloudberries

Major vitamin and mineral content: A, C, calcium, iron, potassium

Look for: undamaged berries with rich amber color; no mold; no caps, stems, or sepals

Refrigerate: Yes. Do not wash until ready to eat.

Freeze: Yes. Spread berries in one layer on a cookie sheet and place in the freezer until completely frozen, then place in an airtight container or plastic bag and freeze for up to a year.

Shelf life: 1 to 2 days in the refrigerator, up to 1 year in the freezer

Cloudberries grow wild in Canada and the northern United States. They are also know as mountain berries, apple berries, and bake-apple berries. They look like raspberries, but are yellow-hued and quite tart. They make excellent preserves. Some berry growers cultivate them, so if you don't see them, ask your grower if he has access to cloudberries. Their unique, wild flavor is worth trying in both sweet and savory recipes.

Corn

Major vitamin and mineral content: A, potassium

Look for: bright green, tight husks; golden silk; plump kernels

Refrigerate: Yes.

Freeze: Yes. Scrape kernels off cob and freeze in an air-tight container.

Shelf life: 1 to 2 days refrigerated, 6 months frozen

Fresh-picked corn on the cob is a quintessential summer food. An American native grass, corn is now grown worldwide and is a staple of many different

Mixed Corn

cuisines. Corn should be eaten the day it's picked because the sugar begins to convert to starch as soon as the ear leaves the stalk. By buying your corn at the farmers' market, rather than the supermarket, you can be more certain of its freshness. Never buy it unhusked. Corn on the cob can be boiled, microwaved, or grilled in its husk and served with fresh butter. Some people prefer white corn, some yellow, some checkerboard—there are countless varieties, and it's simply a matter of personal choice. When you find a type of corn you like, stick with it. Corn can be used in many dishes. Corn pudding is a favorite. Bake fresh corn into muffins, make corn relish or corn chowder. Enjoy the fresh corn of summer while you can get it.

See recipes on pages 130, 136, 140, and 157.

BRENTWOOD CORN

*I*f it's mid-July or August, you'd better get to Oakland's Jack London Square early. If you don't, you might miss out on the best corn in northern California. Brentwood corn sells out as quickly as the growers can get it off their truck. Picked early in the morning in the fields in Brentwood, this corn has a well-deserved reputation for being super-sweet and delicious. Many growers rush to the Brentwood truck before they set up their own stands, just to be sure they get their Brentwood corn. True corn afficionados often come to the farmers' market just for the corn (of course, they usually buy other goodies too).

Northern California's Brentwood is nothing like the swanky and infamous Brentwood section of Los Angeles. Located about an hour or so northwest of San Francisco, it used to be in the heart of a thriving agricultural region. Now it is the last agrarian stronghold against the ever-encroaching urbanization of the greater Bay area.

Cowberries and Lingonberries

Major vitamin and mineral content: C

Look for: firm, deep red berries

Refrigerate: Yes.

Freeze: Yes. Place in an airtight plastic bag.

Shelf life: about 2 months in the refrigerator, at least a year in the freezer

 The cowberry and the lingonberry are wild cousins of the cranberry. Like the cranberry, they are extremely tart. They grow in pastures in Maine and Canada, and you will find them at your farmers' market in the fall if you live in these areas. Homemade cowberry relish for Thanksgiving is a rare treat. Cowberry preserves are also wonderful. Lingonberries make a savory sauce for venison or pheasant, as well as a wonderful juice.

Cranberries

Major vitamin and mineral content: C

Look for: firm, deep red berries that, literally, bounce (an indication of ripeness)

Refrigerate: Yes.

Freeze: Yes. Place in an airtight plastic bag.

Shelf life: about 2 months in the refrigerator, at least a year in the freezer

Extremely tart, cranberries are rich in vitamin C and tradition. They grow in bogs throughout the northern United States and Canada, and you will find them at farmers' markets in the fall if you live in these areas. Homemade cranberry relish for Thanksgiving is a delicious and easy treat. These berries are too tart to eat on their own. They are best when cooked with sugar, honey, or a sweet fruit juice to bring out the flavor and cut the tartness. Or try cranberries instead of blueberries in your favorite muffin recipe.

Cucumber

Major vitamin and mineral content: A, C, calcium, potassium

Look for: firm cucumbers; smooth skin; bright colors; no soft spots

Refrigerate: Yes.

Freeze: No.

Shelf life: about 10 days refrigerated

The cucumber is a refreshing member of the gourd family. It is available in many varieties, the most popular being the regular garden-variety cucumber with seeds, the lemon cucumber (so-called because it is the size and shape of a lemon), the little Kirby, used for pickles, and the seedless English cucumber. They are all usually eaten raw. If you buy organic cukes, you don't have to peel them. Nonorganic ones have most likely been waxed for cosmetic purposes. Try to avoid them. Cucumbers are great in salads and cold soups, or just eaten on their own. Try juicing them for a refreshing summer cooler.

See recipes on pages 140 and 148.

Currants

Major vitamin and mineral content: beta carotene, calcium, potassium, A, C; good source of dietary fiber

Look for: tiny, round, firm berries; brightly colored black, red, or white; stems attached

Refrigerate: Yes. Do not wash until ready to use.

Freeze: Yes, in their boxes and well wrapped.

Shelf-life: 2 days refrigerated and 6 months in the freezer

Fresh currants bear no relation to the more familiar dried currants. They are related to the gooseberry and grow in the more northern areas of our continent. The white and black varieties are very tart and best used in preserves, but the red ones have a pleasing sweet-tart taste that makes them great for eating out of hand for those who like to pucker up. They also make wonderful jams, jellies, and preserves. Currants are showing up more and more at farmers' markets, so start looking.

 Dates

Major vitamin and mineral content: potassium, protein, iron

Look for: plump, soft fruit; shiny skin; no mold or sugar crystals

Refrigerate: Yes. Store in plastic bags.

Freeze: No.

Shelf life: fresh dates, about 2 weeks in the refrigerator; dried dates, up to 6 months in an airtight container at room temperature or up to a year in the refrigerator

Dates, the fruit of the date palm tree, are native to the Middle East but are now grown in many hot desert areas in the United States. If you live in California or the Southwest, you may find fresh dates at your market. Dried Medjool dates are sold at supermarkets everywhere, but at the farmers' market, you will find many varieties, each with its own unique texture and flavor: Barhee, Deglet Noor, Halavie, Medjool, Honey, Dayri, Empress, and Abada. Fresh dates are not as sweet as dried, although they are still about 50 percent sugar. They have an almost persimmon-like flavor and are somewhat juicy. As dates dry, their sugar content increases and they become more creamy than juicy. Dates are very high in calories. They are wonderful in cookies, date-nut bread, and smoothies, or just eaten out of hand. If you have a sweet craving, try a date.

See recipe on page 194.

Eggs: (Clockwise from the top left: Aracuna, Duck, Turkey; Goose)

Major vitamin and mineral content: A, D, protein, riboflavin, choline, phosphorus

Look for: check for cracks and avoid them

Refrigerate: Yes, in the egg carton. Store large end up.

Freeze: Yes. Egg whites and yolks can be frozen separately. Add one-eighth teaspoon of salt to one-quarter cup of yolks before freezing; whites can be frozen in ice cube trays without any additives. Thaw in refrigerator. Do not microwave.

Shelf life: Up to one month refrigerated. For best flavor, use within week of purchase. Up to 6 months frozen

 Chicken, and other fowl eggs have been a staple of many cuisines for centuries. In spite of its high cholesterol (all concentrated in the yolk), the egg is a fantastic nutritional package. You may have

seen eggs labeled "farm fresh" at your supermarket, but chances are those eggs have been sitting on the shelf for a few days. When you buy them at the farmers' market, you can be sure that they truly are fresh from the hen, probably laid that morning. The taste will prove it. There is nothing quite so wonderful as a fluffy omelette made from freshly laid eggs. At the market, you will also find other fowl eggs—from tiny, thimble-sized quail eggs to duck and goose eggs big enough to serve 2 or three people. Many people believe that brown eggs are tastier than white ones. This is simply untrue. Some hens lay brown eggs and some lay white. The eggs are the same in every other way. It is also commonly believed that fertile eggs are more nutritious than non-fertile. Again, this is a myth. Fertile eggs have a small amount of male hormone, and perish more easily. Otherwise, there is no difference. Blood spots on the yolk do not affect quality or flavor, so don't discard them. The quality of eggs at the farmer's market is generally higher than store-bought, and they are always fresher and less expensive.

See recipes on pages 192 and 200.

Eggplant

Major vitamin and mineral content: folic acid, potassium; high in sodium

Look for: firm fruit that is heavy for its size; smooth skin; good color; young eggplants are preferable

Refrigerate: Yes.

Freeze: No.

Shelf life: about 2 days refrigerated

The eggplant, a cousin of the tomato and potato, is really a berry. It comes in all shapes and sizes and can be used in many recipes. The standard deep purple eggplant can be sliced, breaded, and fried. The smaller long thin Japanese eggplants are slightly sweeter and make wonderful eggplant parmesan. Egg-shaped white eggplants are becoming increasingly available. They have a more tender skin and slightly sweeter flesh than other varieties. Eggplant is the key ingredient in baba ganoush, a Middle Eastern dish popular as a dip or appetizer.

See recipe on page 133.

Eggplant: (left: Regular; middle: Japanese; right: Miniature)

*E*ndive

Major vitamin and mineral content: A, C, calcium, iron

Look for: fresh, crisp texture; small, cigar-shaped, white, tightly packed head; no brown spots; as little green as possible

Refrigerate: Yes.

Freeze: No.

Shelf life: 1 day refrigerated. Keep away from light.

 Endive is a highly perishable "green" that is grown indoors, away from light—thus its white color. Although most endive is imported to North America, improved farming methods have made this labor-inten-

Endive

sive vegetable more widely available on these shores, albeit not less expensive. If you have a specialty lettuce grower at your farmers' market, chances are she has some endive for you. Endive has a bittersweet flavor, and can be used in salads or braised lightly with other vegetables. Endive leaves stuffed with fresh goat cheese make wonderful hors d'oeuvres.

See recipe on page 150.

Fava beans

Major vitamin and mineral content: A, C, calcium, potassium

Look for: crisp, firm, large pods; good green color; velvety texture; pods should not bulge with beans

Refrigerate: Yes.

Freeze: No.

Shelf life: 2 days refrigerated

Fava beans, also known as broad beans, are the Mediterranean cousins of the lima and green beans. They have a meaty, classic bean flavor and are

51

delicious in soups and stews, or blanched and served with a nice Chianti. Fava pods are not eaten, and the beans should not be eaten raw. Some people have toxic reactions to them. Unless the beans are very young, favas are practically inedible, so choose with care.

Feijoa

Major vitamin and mineral content: C

Look for: small egg-shaped fruit; slightly soft, bright green skin; sweet aroma

Refrigerate: Ripen at room temperature, then refrigerate.

Freeze: No.

Shelf life: 3 to 5 days in the refrigerator

   The feijoa, also known as pineapple guava, is one of the tropical fruits now being cultivated in the more temperate areas of the United States. Feijoas are native to South America. They have an unsual flavor, something like a tangy strawberry/pineapple blend. They are excellent in fruit salads. Be sure to peel them, for the skin is quite bitter.

Fennel

Major vitamin and mineral content: A, calcium, phosphorus, potassium

Look for: plump, pale, round bulbs; no brown marks; fluffy, feathery tops

Refrigerate: Yes.

Freeze: No.

Shelf life: about 1 week in the refrigerator

This crisp, sweet vegetable comes from Italy, where it is called finocchio. It is often incorrectly referred to as anise, which it is not, even though the taste is similar. You are most likely to find Florence fennel at your farmers' market: It looks like celery on steroids— with a perm. Almost any part of a meal is enhanced by fennel. Serve raw fennel strips with goat cheese as an appetizer or braise it in white wine for a terrific side dish. Since fennel is becoming available in more markets every day, prices are dropping. Try it!

See recipes on pages 134, 160, and 161.

Fiddlehead ferns

Major vitamin and mineral content: A, C

Look for: rich deep green color; small, tightly coiled heads

Refrigerate: Yes.

Freeze: No.

Shelf life: about 2 days refrigerated

 Those on the East Coast have the advantage when it comes to fiddlehead ferns. This musky, chewy vegetable is edible early in the growth stage of the ostrich fern, and its season can be as brief as two weeks. If you see them at your market, buy them. They taste like the forest in springtime. Some people like fiddleheads raw in salads, othes prefer them lightly sautéed or steamed. Caution: Many ferns look like fiddleheads during their early development stage, but are not. Do not try to gather your own ferns in the forest.

See recipes on pages 171 and 172.

Figs (fresh)

Major vitamin and mineral content: calcium, iron, phosphorous

Look for: plump, soft fruit; no bruises or spots

Refrigerate: Yes, but first ripen at room temperature.

Freeze: No.

Shelf life: 1 to 3 days in the refrigerator

Many people think of figs as the dried round things in gift baskets that no one wants to eat. This is because they have never had a fresh, ripe fig. The difference in flavor and consistency is marked. There is per-

Figs

haps no greater sensuous luxury in the plant world than a sweet, succulent fresh fig. The fig is an ancient fruit brought to California from the Mediterranean by Spanish missionaries in the seventeenth century. Now the fig grows all over the continent, thriving anywhere there is a warm summer. When you see figs at your farmers' market in late summer, you'll know that autumn is almost here. Figs come in many varieties and colors, such as Adriatic (green skin), Calimyrna (green), Celeste (purple), Kadota (yellow-green), Brunswick (pink-yellow), and Mission (deep purple). They can be very expensive in supermarkets, because they are so delicate and difficult to ship. You're likely to get better figs at a better price at the farmers' market. Figs are wonderful eaten out of hand, with or without the skin. The seeds are edible too.

See recipe on page 194.

Major vitamin and mineral content: Varies.

Look for: fresh, brightly colored blossoms; no wilting

Refrigerate: Yes.

Freeze: No.

Shelf life: depending on variety, 1 to 3 days refrigerated

    Many flowers are edible, but you should eat only the ones sold by specialty flower farmers who grow them specifically for culinary purposes. Other flowers may have been sprayed with pesticides, and no matter how visually appealing they are, they should never be eaten. Edible flowers can be used as garnishes for drinks and just about any dish, or as part of a salad. You can decorate pastry with them, and you can candy them as well. Some of the more familiar edible flowers are nasturtiums, which have a peppery flavor;

Edible Flowers: (top: Nasturtiums; middle: Johnny-Jump-Up; bottom: Violets)

DUFFIELD FARMS

*S*eattle has one of the finest year-round farmers' markets—the Pike Place Market, overlooking Puget sound and the Olympic Peninsula. Against this gorgeous backdrop, you can find the most delectable berries, the freshest wild salmon, and Judy Duff's chemical-free specialty produce.

Although Seattle is a large city, it is not as far removed from rural areas as most urban centers are. Many of the growers at the Pike Place Market come from farms that are relatively close to downtown Seattle. Judy Duff lives and farms in Burien, a suburb, really, only about a forty-five minute drive from the Market.

Every morning, Judy gets up at about 4:30 and surveys her four acres. She and her daughter pick whatever is market-ready. When you buy produce from Judy at Pike Place, you know it's fresh. With so little acreage, every inch of land counts. Judy and her daughter grow small crops of edible flowers like borage, Johnny-Jump-ups, bachelor-buttons, and other floral delicacies. She also farms specialty lettuces and herbs and is famous for her fresh morels and soybeans. The day I visited her in Seattle, she had beautiful red and golden raspberries at her abundant stall in the Market.

Judy Duff and Duffield Farms, her "family business," represent the best of what you can find by shopping at a local farmers' market: growers who know their products—from seed and soil to sellers' table—and a commitment to quality in everything they grow.

Duffield Farms
Box 66925
Seattle, WA 98166

pansies, which have a grapey taste; squash or zucchini blossoms, which can be stuffed and deep-fried; and chive blossoms, which have a gentle, oniony flavor. There are many varieties of edible flowers. They are usually grown in hothouses, so if you have a year-round farmers'market, you'll be able to add some beautiful color to your dishes even in the heart of winter.

See recipe on page 177.

Major vitamin and mineral content: depends on fruit

Look for: no mold; no sulfites (ask if necessary)

Refrigerate: Yes, but not necessary.

Freeze: No.

Shelf life: at least 6 months in an airtight container in a cool, dry place

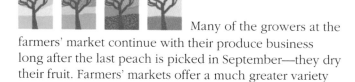 Many of the growers at the farmers' market continue with their produce business long after the last peach is picked in September—they dry their fruit. Farmers' markets offer a much greater variety

Dried Fruit: (clockwise from top left: Apricots, Figs, Cherries, Prunes; Pears)

of dried fruits than supermarkets. You may find everything from dried figs and dates to dried peaches and
pears. In many cases, the farmers' dried fruit is not treated with sulfites, as is done in many food processing
plants to prevent spoilage. If you store your dried fruit
properly, you will not need to fear spoilage. Dried cherries or cranberries added to a salad with a light vinaigrette and some sunflower seeds make a great appetizer.
Try substituting different dried fruits in any recipe that
calls for dried fruit. Or add chopped dried apples, apricots,
and nectarines to your trail mix. In general, most dried
fruits are sweeter than fresh fruits, because the water content is almost nil, and so the sugar and flavor become
intensified. For example, a fresh cranberry is too tart too
eat, but a dried one is quite tasty. Note: Dried currants
are not the dried version of fresh currants. They are dried
Zantë or champagne grapes—simply small raisins.

See recipes on pages 182, 187, and 188.

Garlic

Major vitamin and mineral content: It's good for you!

Look for: Elephant and white garlic: tight, firm, fat bulbs;
no soft spots; no sprouting. Green garlic: should look like
small leeks, without any developed cloves

Refrigerate: No.

Freeze: No.

Shelf life: at least 2 months in a cool, dry place

    Garlic

 Green garlic

A kitchen just isn't a kitchen without fresh garlic. At your
market, you'll find the most common, white American,
and the gigantic, exotic elephant garlic. Although elephant garlic is a California native, other growers around
the country are giving it a try. In the spring, be sure to
pick up green garlic if you see it. It is young garlic that
has yet to form cloves. It has a softer, sweeter flavor than
other garlic. Garlic is thought to have medicinal qualities,
and many people take supplements every day. Garlic also
inspires an almost religious fervor. Next time you visit

Garlic: (top: White; middle: Pink; bottom: Green)

California, try to have your trip coincide with the Gilroy Garlic Festival, where you can join about one hundred thousand people in the worship of the "stinking rose." Tasting garlic wine, garlic ice cream, and even some traditional recipes, such as garlic pesto, are just some of the activities of this famous festival.

See recipes on pages 131, 150, 171, and 180.

Ginger

Major vitamin and mineral content: potassium

Look for: Young ginger: translucent, thin skin; lightly colored shoots. Mature ginger: plump rhizomes with few knobs; smooth skin; spicy fragrance

Refrigerate: Yes.

Freeze: Yes.

Shelf life: up to 2 weeks refrigerated, 2 months in the freezer

Fresh ginger has a spicy, fresh, sharp flavor that is usually absent from ground dried ginger. It adds wonderful flavor to many dishes, from desserts to meat marinades. Young ginger doesn't need to be peeled, and it is quite mild. Mature ginger has a thick skin and a stronger flavor; it should be peeled. Both kinds can be used in any recipe calling for ginger. One tablespoon of fresh ginger, minced, grated, or sliced, equals about one-eighth teaspoon of dried. Besides adding great flavor to just about any recipe, ginger is thought to aid in digestion.

See recipes on pages 182 and 199.

Gooseberries

Major vitamin and mineral content: calcium, potassium, A, C, beta carotene

Look for: firm, furry berries with uniform color; no mold

Refrigerate: Yes. Do not wash until ready to use.

Freeze: No.

Shelf life: 2 days in the refrigerator

Gooseberries are larger, fuzzier cousins of fresh currants. They are too tart to eat on their own, but they make wonderful pies, jams, and preserves and are the key ingredient in a traditional British dessert called a fool. If you have a specialty berry grower at your market, chances are he'll have gooseberries. Give them a try.

Grapefruit

Major vitamin and mineral content: calcium, potassium, A, C, beta carotene

Look for: round, yellow fruit that feels heavy for its size; spongy flesh, but not too soft; smooth skin

Refrigerate: Yes.

Freeze: No.

Shelf life: up to 2 weeks refrigerated

Grapefruit: (top: Pink; bottom: White)

 Grapefruit, packed with vitamin C, is everyone's favorite breakfast fruit. Different kinds of grapefruits have different qualities. White ones have white skin and whitish-yellow flesh. Pink have yellow skins, sometimes with a pink blush, and flesh that can be anywhere from light pink to dark red. Red grapefruits contain more vitamin A than other kinds. There is no general rule to choosing a sweet grapefruit. Just try the ones that look and feel good. Usually they are available year-round.

See recipe on page 195.

Grapes

Major vitamin and mineral content: A, C, calcium, potassium

Look for: plump firm fruit attached to stems; uniform color

Refrigerate: Yes.

Grapes: (top: Red; middle: Champagne; bottom: Green)

Freeze: No.

Shelf life: up to a week refrigerated, depending on variety

There are thousands of varieties of grapes, from the tiny dark pink Zantë grape, which is dried to make dried currants, to the famous green Thompson seedless, found in every produce section of every supermarket in North America. At your farmers' market, you may find many varieties that are not ordinarily sold commercially. If you live in a wine-producing region, you may find cabernet, zinfandel, or chardonnay grapes. These are not as sweet as table grapes and make interesting additions to recipes that call for grapes. Other table grapes, both seedless and seeded, come in many colors, from pale green to deep purple, and often can only be found locally, since only the hardiest ship well. The freshly picked grapes rushed to your farmers' market have never been refrigerated and have an entirely different flavor from those you find at the supermarket. Grapes make great snacks, jellies, juice, and pies.

See recipe on page 150.

Green beans

Major vitamin and mineral content: A, C, calcium, potassium

Look for: small to medium-sized pods; no wilting or wrinkling; tender enough to eat raw, but very crisp; pods should not be rubbery

Refrigerate: Yes.

Freeze: Yes. Blanch and store in an airtight container.

Shelf life: up to 5 days refrigerated, 6 months in the freezer

 Fresh green beans, also known as string or snap beans, come in several varieties. If you have fresh beans available at your market, there's no reason ever to buy frozen or canned again! Fresh green beans are one of life's simple pleasures. Among the more commonly found varieties are Kentucky Wonder, Baby Blue Lake, haricots verts, and Chinese long beans. They are best served raw in a salad or vinaigrette, or lightly blanched or sautéed.

See recipe on page 134, 154, and 161.

Greens

Major vitamin and mineral content: A, C, calcium, iron, potassium

Look for: crisp-looking leaves and stalks; no wilting; bright green or green with red color; no yellowing

Refrigerate: Yes.

Freeze: No.

Shelf life: 2 days refrigerated

Greens: (clockwise from top: Beet, Collard, Dandelion, Mustard)

Greens are becoming more popular as people eat more vegetables and look for variety in their diet. Greens, as defined here, are the edible leaves of certain plants that can be eaten raw or cooked. Although there are many kinds, most require similar treatment in cooking. Among the greens you'll find at your farmers' market are beet greens, collards, kale, spinach, turnip greens, mustard greens, and dandelion greens. Mustard, dandelion greens, and, sometimes spinach, are best raw mixed into salads, but the other kinds of greens improve with cooking. Be sure to wash all greens thoroughly. They can be sandy.

See recipe on page 144.

Guava

Major vitamin and mineral content: A, C, beta carotene, calcium

Look for: firm fruit; no spots; sweet aroma

Refrigerate: Yes, but ripen at room temperature first.

Freeze: No.

Shelf life: 2 to 3 days in the refrigerator

Guavas are a sweet, delicate tropical fruit that is being grown more and more in the warmer parts of North America. Its skin color can be anything from yellow to red to deep purple, and its flesh ranges from yellow to ruby red. Guavas make a great addition to smoothies and other fresh fruit drinks.

Hazelnuts

Major vitamin and mineral content: calcium, potassium

Look for: clean, uncracked shells; nuts should not rattle when you shake them

Refrigerate: Yes, in an airtight container.

Freeze: Yes, in an airtight container.

Shelf life: about 4 months refrigerated, 10 months to 1 year in the freezer

Hazelnuts, also known as filberts, have been grown in the United States only since the 1940s. Since then, they have become a staple in many pantries. They are relatively sweet, compared to other nuts, and are used in making desserts and candies. Before using, be sure to remove the bitter-tasting skin. Hazelnuts can also be delicious in savory dishes. Try them in stuffing instead of chestnuts.

See recipe on page 195.

Herbs: (clockwise from top center: Rosemary;Thyme; Oregano; Basil; Cilantro; Sage; Dill;Tarragon; Parsley)

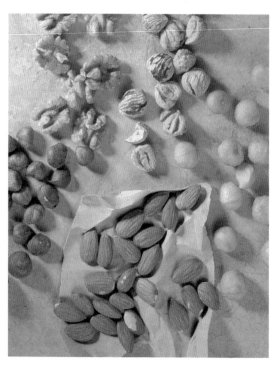

Nuts: (clockwise from top right: Chestnuts, Macadamia Nuts,Almonds, Hazelnuts,Walnuts)

Major vitamin and mineral content: N/A

Look for: Fresh herbs: fragrant herbs; bright color; no wilting or mold. Dried herbs: thoroughly dried but fragrant herbs

Refrigerate: Fresh, yes; dried, no.

Freeze: Yes, just fresh.

Shelf life: Fresh: 2 to 5 days refrigerated, up to 6 months frozen; dried: up to 6 months in an airtight container, away from light

 Fresh bay leaves, chamomile, chervil, chives, epazote, lemon balm, yarrow, borage, basil, cilantro, dill, lovage, marjoram, mint, oregano, parsley, rosemary, sage, tarragon, thyme—the variety of fresh and dried herbs at your farmers' market is unlimited. Familiar herbs, like oregano, are there in abundance, but so are the more exotic ones, like epazote and lemon balm. Fresh herbs purchased at the farmers' market are much fresher than herbs bought at the supermarket, and they usually have not been treated with pesticides. Their flavor is wonderful. If you use dried herbs, it is also preferable to buy them at the farmers' market, since they are usually fresher. No one knows how long those supermarket dried herbs have been sitting on the shelf in their glass bottles, or what kinds of chemicals they've been treated with. Talk to the grower about what you can do with herbs that are unfamiliar to you. Many herbs have medicinal as well as culinary value. As you become acquainted with new herbs, you will get to know their qualities well, and will be able to try new recipes with new flavors.

See recipes on pages 128, 132, 136, 142, 143, 152, 156, 159, 160, 162, 164, 178, 180, and 181.

 ickory nuts

Major vitamin and mineral content: iron, phosporous, thiamine

Look for: hard, uncracked shells

Refrigerate: No.

COACH DAIRY GOAT FARM

*L*illian and Miles Cahn first established Coach Dairy Goat Farm in 1984, and the undertaking has developed beyond their wildest imaginations.

Previously owners of Coach Leather, the Cahn's sold this business and bought a farm located in Pine Plains, a small Hudson Valley Village, just two hours outside of New York City. They began with 200 French Alpine dairy goats and have grown to over 900 goats, born and raised on their farm. The small white-tiled creamery where the cheeses are made connects directly to the milking parlor.

The farm consists of some 700 acres just to provide the goats with the feed and bedding they require. The Cahn's have donated a special easement to the Columbia County Land Conservancy which will ensure that this beautiful property remains unspoiled, open farmland forever.

Coach Farm produces a whole line of goat cheeses, both fresh and aged in different sizes and shapes—discs, logs, buttons, medallions, bricks, cones, hearts, wheels, and reduced fat sticks. They also have a line of goat's milk yogurt.

Coach Farm products are so special because they are made from Grade A goat's milk that gives them a clean, fresh taste without any of the unpleasant "goatiness" found in so many of the other goat cheeses. They are made right on the farm, in small, carefully-tended batches and hand-ladled into draining molds.

If you walk into the Union Square Farmers' Market in New York City on any given Friday or Saturday you will find a Coach Farm stand with cheeses wrapped in special papers that enable the live cultures to breathe and the cheese to stay fresh. They have not been allowed to go stale, sealed up for months in plastic vacuum packages. There are no stabilizers, preservatives, artificial ingredients, or additives of any kind. Just friendly faces, such as the Cahns' daughter Susie, working at the Market to help you choose the goat cheese or yogurt that is right for you.

The Coach Dairy Goat Farm
RR 1 Box 445
Pine Plains, NY 12567
518-398-5325

See recipe on page 132.

Freeze: No.

Shelf life: in the shell, at least 6 months in an airtight container in a cool, dry place

Hickory nuts are native to North America. They have a very hard shell, and you may need a hammer to get at the nutmeat—but it's worth it. They have a rich, buttery flavor and can be used in dessert recipes in place of pecans. They are very high in fat and are usually sold in the shell.

Horseradish

Major vitamin and mineral content: A, potassium

Look for: very hard root; no soft spots or blemishes

Refrigerate: Yes, wrapped in paper.

Freeze: Yes.

Shelf life: up to 8 weeks in the refrigerator, 6 months in the freezer

Horseradish

Horseradish root is extremely pungent and should be used in moderation. It can be grated and used in sauces or as a condiment. Fresh horseradish has a much sharper flavor than store-bought prepared horseradish.

See recipe on page 172.

Jerusalem artichokes

Major vitamin and mineral content: iron

Look for: firm roots; no soft spots

Refrigerate: Yes.

Freeze: No.

Shelf life: up to 2 weeks in the refrigerator

Jerusalem artichokes, also called sunchokes, are not artichokes and have no relationship to Jerusalem. These North American natives are part of the

Jerusalem Artichokes

sunflower family. They have a crunchy texture and a sweet, nutty flavor. You don't need to peel them; the skin is very nutritious. Just be sure to wash them thoroughly They are great raw in salads and make a good, crunchy addition to crudités platters. You can prepare them like potatoes for an interesting side dish.

Jícama

Major vitamin and mineral content: C, potassium

Look for: hard flesh; unblemished skin

Refrigerate: Yes.

Freeze: No.

Shelf life: 1 week in the refrigerator

   Jícama, also known as a Mexican potato, is a crunchy Mexican root vegetable that is delicious eaten raw or cooked. It is now grown north of the border, and you may find it at your market, especially if you live in an area with a Latino population. It looks like a cross between an Idaho potato and a hard squash. Try adding raw jícama strips to a mixed green salad with a balsamic vinaigrette, or add jícama strips to a crudités platter. When cooked, it remains crispy and makes an interesting side dish.

Kale

Major vitamin and mineral content: A, C, calcium, folic acid, iron, good source of dietary fiber

Look for: Vivid colors (purple, green, lavender, blue tints); crispy leaves; no wilting

Refrigerate: Yes.

Freeze: No.

Shelf life: up to 3 days refrigerated

   Kale is a member of the cabbage family. You may have seen it growing in gardens as an ornamental plant, but it is wonderfully edible as well. It originated

Kale

in Europe, and was one of the first plants brought to North America by early immigrants. It has a mild, cabbage-like flavor, and is a well-liked, nutritious winter vegetable. It is best prepared in any way you would spinach—steam, sauté, even use it in a vegetable cream soup. Small amounts of raw kale make an interesting addition to a salad. Like spinach, kale can be very gritty and sandy, so be sure to wash it thoroughly before using.

Kiwifruit

Major vitamin and mineral content: C, E, folic acid, potassium

Look for: firm fruit; no wrinkles, cuts, or bruises

Refrigerate: Yes, but ripen at room temperature first. Store in the refrigerator away from other fruits because the kiwi may cause your other produce to become over-ripe.

Freeze: Yes. Remove excess fuzz and freeze whole.

Shelf life: up to 2 weeks refrigerated

these American natives another chance by trying fresh ones from your farmers' market. Fresh beans have an entirely different flavor—a fresher taste, a better consistency. There are two major varieties of lima beans, Fordhook and baby lima. Fordhooks are larger and more flavorful.

*L*ime

Major vitamin and mineral content: C

Look for: firm fruit; smooth skin; fruit that is heavy for its size; good green color

Refrigerate: Yes.

Freeze: The juice can be frozen.

Shelf life: about 2 weeks refrigerated

Limes are almost as versatile as lemons. From limeade to margaritas, marinades to seviches, limes

Limes

can be used in almost any recipe that calls for lemon juice or vinegar. If you live in Florida, you may have a grower who sells Key limes. These are slightly smaller than Persian limes (the most common kind) and have more of a yellow tinge. They are the key ingredient in Key lime pie.

See recipe on page 186.

*L*itchis

Major vitamin and mineral content: C, potassium

Look for: small fruit (1″–2″); bright red shell; rough skin with no blemishes

Refrigerate: Yes. Unshell before refrigerating.

Freeze: No.

Shelf life: up to one week refrigerated

Litchis are a Chinese fruit that has only recently begun to be cultivated in the more tropical areas of North

Litchis

America. Because of their rarity and short season, fresh litchis are considered a delicacy. Their juicy flesh has a sweet, custardy flavor. They make a wonderful addition to fruit salads and fruit desserts. They can also be eaten out of hand—just shell and seed. Dried litchis are available year-round, and are called litchi nuts. These are mostly imports, so it is doubtful that you will come across them at your farmers' market. Eat them like any other snack.

Loquats

Major vitamin and mineral content: potassium

Look for: large fruit; tender skin; sweet aroma; apricot color

Refrigerate: No.

Freeze: No.

Shelf life: 2 days at room temperature

  Florida

   California

The loquat comes from China, but it is sometimes called a Japanese plum. The juicy, crisp fruit has a sweet-tart flavor and is considered a rare delicacy. Loquats can be eaten out of hand or used in poultry dishes. Since they are extremely fragile, you will only find them in the regions where they are grown.

Macadamia nuts

Major vitamin and mineral content: potassium, calcium

Look for: plump, crisp nuts

Refrigerate: No.

Freeze: No.

Shelf life: up to 6 months in an airtight container in a cool, dark place

 Macadamia nuts are native to Australia but have long been grown in Hawaii, where they still thrive as one of that state's largest exports. On the mainland, macadamias are starting to be cultivated in the more temperate regions. You may find them at your farmers' market at a good price. Since they keep well if stored properly, they are available year-round. They are usually sold shelled and roasted, with or without salt. They are sweet, rich, and buttery and very high in fat. But if you find them at your market, indulge.

Mandarin oranges

Major vitamin and mineral content: C, beta-carotene

Look for: firm fruit; bright color; glossy skin; fruit that is heavy for its size

Refrigerate: Yes.

Freeze: The juice can be frozen.

Shelf life: 1 week at room temperature, up to 4 weeks in the refrigerator

The name Mandarin orange actually refers to an entire group of loose-skinned oranges. Tangerines and tangelos are the best known. Others include satsuma, clementine, Mineola, Dancy, and Murcott. All of these sweet citrus fruits are easy to peel and make for great eating out of hand. Most growers will let you taste the various kinds so you can choose your favorite. When tangerines are in season, juice them in the morning instead of oranges. Satsumas in particular make great snacks. They have almost no seeds and even the skin is edible (if the fruit is organic). Most Mandarin oranges are smaller than regular oranges.

Mango

Major vitamin and mineral content: A, C, D

Look for: unblemished, yellow skin with a pink blush; large fruit; sweet aroma

Refrigerate: No.

Freeze: Yes. Peel, seed, and cube the fruit and place in an airtight container.

Shelf life: 1 to 2 days at room temperature, 3 to 4 months in the frezer

 Mangoes, originally from India, are now cultivated in more temperate areas of North America and can be found at some farmers' markets. The sweet, juicy, aromatic fruit surrounds a large seed, so buy the larger fruits—you'll get more flesh relative to seed. They are best eaten out of hand or made into chutney.

See recipe on page 183.

Mint

Major vitamin and mineral content: N/A

Look for: vividly colored leaves; no wilting

Refrigerate: Yes. Place, stems down, in a glass of water and cover with a plastic bag. Change water every 2 days.

Mint: (clockwise from top left: Spearmint, Blue Balsam, Huron Balm)

Freeze: Not recommended. To preserve mint, it is best to dry it and place in an airtight container.

Shelf life: up to 1 week refrigerated; up to 6 months dried

 Mint grows wild all over the world, and there are over forty known varieties of the herb. Peppermint and spearmint are the most popular and familiar. Your herb grower at the farmers' market will be able to introduce you to some of the more exotic mints, like lemon mint and chocolate mint. She will also supply you with the freshest peppermint and spearmint. Fresh mint grows best in summer, but it is cultivated year-round in greenhouses all over North America, so you should have no problem finding it. Any recipe, sweet or savory, that calls for mint will be improved a thousand-fold by using fresh mint. A mint julep is simply no good without muddled fresh mint. What would a leg of lamb be without mint sauce or jelly? Because of its ubiquity, many cultures use mints in their cuisines. Chances are you will find recipes that include mints if you look into any of the cuisines of Asia, Europe and North America.

See recipe on page 145.

Mushroom

Major vitamin and mineral content: potassium

Look for: firm mushrooms; no broken caps; no dry spots; should have a good musky aroma

Refrigerate: Yes.

Freeze: No.

Shelf life: from 2 days to 1 week in the refrigerator, depending on variety

 The market for mush-rooms has mushroomed! You no longer need be restricted to the bland little button variety, when countless varieties of exotic wild and cultivated mushrooms await you at your farmers' market. Grill some meaty portobellos with olive oil, toss some enokis or shiitakes into your stir-fry or stew. Search out the chanterelle, the lobster, the

Mushrooms: (clockwise from top left: Shiitake; Morel; American; Portobello; Enoki)

wood ear, the fabled morel! Make friends with your mushroom grower and you will learn the secrets of this fabulous fungus. Some mushrooms are thought to have medicinal qualities. Most kinds are available year-round because of modern growing methods.

See recipes on pages 135, 161, 166.

Muskmelons

Major vitamin and mineral content: N/A

Look for: deep, sweet aroma; firm surface that gives slightly at the blossom end; no mold or fruit flies; fruit that is heavy for its size

Refrigerate: Yes.

Freeze: Yes. Peel and cube the fruit and place in an airtight container.

Shelf life: 1 week in the refrigerator, up to 6 months in the freezer

Melons: (clockwise from top: Crenshaw, Santa Claus, Cavaillon, Cantaloupe, Honeydew, Golden Honeydew)

Cantaloupes, Sharilyns, Galias, honeydews, Casabas, and Persian melons are just some of the fragrant members of the muskmelon family. All muskmelons, unlike watermelons, have seeds in the center of the fruit. Some have netted skins (cantaloupes) and some are smooth-skinned (honeydews). Melon growers in North America are going beyond the cantaloupe these days and are experimenting with all kinds of wonderful, exotic melons. The best place to sample these is at your local farmers' market. To see if a melon is ripe, shake it. If the seeds rattle, it is ready to be eaten. Try a Sharlyn or Galia, which can be delicious and beautiful. They come in many different colors and sizes. Smaller melons make wonderful light desserts when halved, seeded, and filled with raspberry or kiwi sorbet. Slices of the larger members of the family make a great appetizer draped with paper-thin slices of prosciutto and garnished with fresh mint sprigs.

See recipes on pages 145 and 192.

Major vitamin and mineral content: A, C, potassium; good source of dietary fiber

Look for: sweet aroma; rich yellow skin with red blush; slight give at stem end

Refrigerate: Yes, but first ripen at room temperature in a brown paper bag.

Freeze: Slice and sprinkle with lemon juice, then freeze in an airtight container.

Shelf life: 3 to 5 days in the refrigerator, 6 months in the freezer

 "I would rather have a rotten nectarine than a fine plum," said Mel Brooks's 2000-Year-Old Man, and many of us would agree. Even old, gnarly nectarines buried in the refrigerator can make us salivate. Their flavor endures. The nectarine is not "half a peach, half a plum," but a firmer, smooth relative of the peach. There are countless varieties, and color and size varies. Like the peach, the nectarine is one of the ultimate summer fruits. Nothing beats a juicy nectarine for a snack on a hot afternoon. You may see nectarines at your farmers' market as early as May, but wait until July and August for peak flavor. Taste, smell, and then stock up. What you don't eat, you can freeze. Use nectarines in any recipe that calls for peaches.

See recipe on page 201.

$\mathscr{O}$kra

Major vitamin and mineral content: A, C, beta carotene, calcium, folic acid, potassium; good source of dietary fiber

Look for: small, firm pods with good green color; pods that snap easily; no brown spots

Refrigerate: Yes. Do not wash until ready to use.

Freeze: Blanch, then freeze in airtight containers.

Shelf life: 3 to 5 days refrigerated

Okra

Okra is usually thought of as a Southern vegetable, but it is grown all over the country. As the interest in regional cuisine continues to broaden, fresh okra is becoming increasingly available at farmers' markets. Okra is a relative of the cotton plant and was brought to these shores by slaves from Africa. It is an essential ingredient in many Southern dishes, especially gumbo. In some places, in fact, okra is called gumbo, a Creole adaptation of the Bantu word *ngombo*. For many, okra is an acquired taste. The slimy texture of cooked okra can be off-putting, but the asparagus-eggplant-like flavor is quite appealing. Many people have not had fresh okra prepared properly. Okra can be coated in cornmeal, used as a flavorful thickener in stews, or added to a ratatouille. Pickled okra is a crunchy treat. And good filé gumbo is a life-enhancing experience.

Major vitamin and mineral content: C, potassium

Look for: bulbs that are heavy for their size; dry, shiny, papery skins; no soft spots; no sprouting; no mold

Refrigerate: Not recommended.

Freeze: No.

Shelf life: up to 3 months in a cool, dark, dry place; do not store with potatoes

 Bermuda

 Spanish

 Red, Italian

 Maui

 Vidalia

 Walla Walla

 Pearl

 Yellow globe

 Torpedo

 White

Onions: (top: Green; middle right: Pearl; middle left: Vidalia; bottom: Miniature Red)

Dry onions are a staple of any pantry. These are not dried, dehydrated onions, they are simply mature **green onions** that have a dry, papery skin. The most common variety is the yellow globe, but there are many kinds of onions. You will almost certainly find unique onions at your farmers' market. As you experiment with different kinds, you will see which onions suit which recipes best.

See recipes on pages 147, 154, 155, and 173.

Onions, green

Major vitamin and mineral content: A, potassium

Look for: crisp, bright green tops; firm white base

Refrigerate: Yes.

Freeze: No.

Shelf life: about 1 week refrigerated

Shallots

Green onions are a group of immature onions that have not yet developed bulbs. Best known are the scallion, the leek, the chive, and the shallot. But in the springtime, you may find ramps at your farmers' market. These are wild leeks and are quite wonderful in any recipe that calls for a green onion. Green onions have a milder flavor than mature **dry onions** and add a zesty fresh flavor to salads, stews, and chiles. Potato-leek soup is truly sublime on a cold winter's night, and instantly refreshing when chilled for vichyssoise.

See recipes on pages 137, 146, 168, 172, and 176.

SMOKED SALMON
from Cap'n Mike

*M*ichael Hiebert grew up in Dinuba, California, in the heart of the hot and dusty San Joaquin Valley. His father grew grapes and oranges and produced raisins and wine. But Michael did not become a farmer. Always a "surfer boy" at heart, he found himself drawn to the ocean.

While a sales representative for Melitta, he found himself traveling all over the United States and Canada. He was particularly drawn to the Pacific Northwest. He discovered wonderful smoked salmon during a trip to the San Juan Islands, off Canada and southern Washington State. He wondered why he couldn't find smoked fish of the same quality in the San Francisco Bay Area, his home base. He decided to do something about it.

Hiebert studied the very ancient and traditional art of smoking fish at the source: He lived with and learned from the Snohomish and Hoh Indians in Washington State, smoking fish by a river on handmade wooden racks over alderwood covered with deerskins. When he returned to his home in Redwood City, his hobby quickly became an obsession. He started smoking salmon in his backyard, at first for himself, and then for his neighbors. One Sunday, he took about thirty pounds of smoked salmon to the Redwood City Farmers' Market, and sold out within the first hour. He quickly realized he had something people wanted.

For about two years, Hiebert stayed in Redwood City, smoking salmon in his backyard and selling to markets around the Bay Area. However, his love of his work and the demand for his salmon grew to the point where he needed larger facilities. He decided to buy a salmon boat, and he moved to Bodega Bay. He set up his business, Northwest Connection and Cap'n Mike's Smoked Specialties, and a smokehouse facility in Cotati. He was soon catching his own wild salmon and smoking and packaging it at his smokehouse.

Smoking salmon is very labor intensive. It takes about twenty hours to make Northwest Connection's signature alderwood-smoked salmon, and two to three days to make Northwest-style lox. Smoking preserves the natural omega-3 oils in the fish, a good source of polyunsaturated fat. It is not heavily salted—Hiebert says that smoked foods don't have to be salty. He uses only enough salt to make the brine right and works hard to ensure that his products can be enjoyed by everyone, even people on low-sodium diets.

He and his wife, Sally, now sell at about ten markets each week and have expanded their repertoire to salmon jerky, lox, albacore tuna, steelhead trout, and sturgeon. When it's Dungeness crab season, they smoke crabs. They've tried just about everything, from abalone to eels to potato chips (all delicious). They do a brisk mail-order business year-round. Northwest Connection has many fans around the world who first bought smoked salmon while visiting the Bay Area and then discovered they couldn't find anything like it at home. They even ship to Washington State and New York City, two bastions of smoked fish. Hiebert has developed smoked salmon sticks, a kind of pepperoni-like snack made with salmon and spices in a vegetarian casing. His salmon spread is well known throughout the markets. Many farmers trade produce for it so they can have a gourmet breakfast of salmon spread on a fresh sourdough baguette (baked by one of the bread vendors.)

Hiebert uses only alderwood to smoke his fish. It is native to the Pacific Northwest and has been used for centuries for this purpose. He says "alder is to salmon as French oak is to Chardonnay." He has tried other woods, but simply cannot achieve the marvelous flavor that alder imparts to the fish. He is unique in his use of the wood. Most of the smoked salmon one sees in supermarkets, or even on the docks, has been cured in bottled liquid smoke and has never been near a smoker. The difference in taste is remarkable.

Smoked salmon is versatile. Michael and Sally use it instead of smoked ham or bacon in many recipes. Sally's salmon chowder is quite wonderful. As Hiebert says, "The salmon wants you to honor it. Become the salmon and it will tell you its secrets." Michael Hiebert has listened well.

Michael and Sally Hiebert, Owner
Northwest Connection
North Coast Smoked Food Specialties
591 Mercantile Drive Suite 6
Cotati, CA 94931
707-792-0531

See recipes on pages 132 and 179.

Oranges: (top: Valencia; bottom: Blood)

Major vitamin and mineral content: A, C, calcium, potassium, beta carotene

Look for: firm, glossy skin; fruit that is heavy for its size; no mold; slight blemishes or brown spots are OK; sweet aroma

Refrigerate: If necessary.

Freeze: The juice can be frozen.

Shelf life: about 5 days at room temperature, 2 weeks in the refrigerator

 Because oranges are available year-round in supermarkets from coast to coast, it is difficult to remember that they, like all fruits, have a season. Although they are synonymous with sunshine, oranges are not summer fruits. Their peak time is midwinter, though you may find fresh oranges in November or well into April. If you live in Texas, Florida, or California, you will be able to take advantage of fresh-picked oranges at your farmers' market. You haven't really eaten an orange until you've had one picked only hours earlier. Oranges are noted for their vitamin C, but in fact, they contain more vitamin A. There are many varieties of oranges. Navels are the most popular for snacking. They are sweet and easy to peel, and they have no seeds. Best for juicing are Valencia oranges. Blood oranges, popular in the Mediterranean, have been a rarity in the United States, but now they are being grown in greater quantities. They have a reddish-orange skin, and their flesh is a deep ruby red. They can be tart to very sweet; the only way to tell is to taste them. They are wonderful in salads. Try sliced blood oranges with slices of fresh fennel in a raspberry vinaigrette. Squeeze some blood orange juice into your regular orange juice for a gourmet breakfast drink.

See recipes on pages 147 and 169.

Papaya

Major vitamin and mineral content: A, C, calcium, potassium, beta carotene; good source of dietary fiber

Look for: yellow-orange or peach-colored fruit; skin that gives slightly; musky aroma

Refrigerate: No.

Freeze: No.

Shelf life: once ripe, 1 to 3 days at room tempaerature

The papaya is another tropical fruit that is now being grown in temperate regions of North America. You may find the Solo variety at your farmers' market. Its flesh is sweet and smooth, and the peppery seeds are edible. Eat papaya like melon; just halve and scoop.

Parsnip

Major vitamin and mineral content: C, iron

Look for: firm, small to medium roots

Refrigerate: Yes.

Freeze: No.

Shelf life: about 4 weeks refrigerated

Parsnips

Parsnips look like white carrots. They are quite tangy when raw, but can be prepared many different ways. The sweetest, tastiest parsnips show up at the market after the first frost, or even a hard freeze. Treat them like carrots or potatoes. They are excellent in stews, or pureed with carrots as an alternative to mashed potatoes.

See recipes on pages 153 and 163.

Passion fruit

Major vitamin and mineral content: A, C, potassium, beta carotene

Look for: dark purple fruit; puckered, wrinkled skin with no cracks; fruit that is heavy for its size

Refrigerate: Yes, but first ripen at room temperature.

Freeze: Puree the flesh and freeze, or freeze whole.

Shelf life: up to 1 week in the refrigerator, 6 months in the freezer

This South American native is now being grown in our Southeastern states and California. The somewhat unattractive tropical fruit has gelatinous flesh packed with intensely sweet, juicy, aromatic flavor and edible seeds. The skin is inedible; scoop out the pulp and seeds and stir into plain yogurt. Add the juice to drinks or use to make a sorbet.

Peaches

Major vitamin and mineral content: A, C, D, potassium

Look for: firm fruit, with a slight give at the stem area; soft and flowery aroma; no bruises; good yellow or white color

Refrigerate: Not recommended—their flavor and juiciness fades with refrigeration.

Freeze: Yes. Slice and store in an airtight container.

Shelf life: once ripe, 2 to 3 days at room temperature

Peaches are perhaps the quintessential summer fruit. Biting into a perfect peach is just about as good as it gets. There are countless varieties of peaches. Try different ones until you find the one (or ones) for you. Ask the farmer for a taste and see what you think. Peaches should be ready to eat when you buy them since they do not ripen well off the tree. If you want to remember the wonder of a warm summer day in the midst of a bleak February, start canning and preserving peaches in mid-August, or sooner. Some varieties are only available at the beginning of the summer, so if you're a peach aficionado, canning or preserving may be an ongoing summer project.

See recipe on page 198.

Pear

Major vitamin and mineral content: A, phosphorus

Look for: firm but aromatic fruit; no blemishes

Refrigerate: Yes, but first ripen at room temperature in a paper bag.

Freeze: Yes. Slice and dip in lemon water before freezing. Canning is preferable.

Shelf life: 3 to 7 days refrigerated, depending on variety

 There are countless varieties of pears, but one thing they all have in common is that they should not be ripe when you buy them. Pears improve in texture and flavor after they've been picked. Bartlett, Bosc, and Anjou pears are the most common varieties grown in North America, but you may find specialty or heritage fruit such as Comice, Seckel, Red Bartlett, Clapp's, Forelle, Nelis, and French Butter at your farmers' market. Try different kinds. Pears can be spicy and sweet, aromatic, or tangy. They are excellent for poaching, making into preserves and tarts, or just eating out of hand.

See recipe on page 149.

Peas

Major vitamin and mineral content: A, potassium

Look for: bright green pods

Refrigerate: Yes.

Freeze: Yes. Shell, then freeze in airtight containers.

Shelf life: 1 to 2 days refrigerated, 6 months frozen

 Fresh English, or garden, peas are the best-known member of the pea branch of the legume family. Look for the lovely green pods starting in the spring. Shell the peas and eat them the same day. Fresh peas are a treat. Just steam or boil them briefly, and serve with a dab of sweet butter. Or even better, just eat them raw, out of hand.

Peas: (top: Sugar Snap; middle: Snow; bottom left: English)

Pears: (clockwise from top: Bartlett, Comice, Bosc)

Major vitamin and mineral content: potassium

Look for: clean, unblemished shells; no cracks; nuts should not rattle when shaken

Refrigerate: Yes.

Freeze: Yes, shell and freeze in an airtight container.

Shelf life: up to 2 months at room temperature, 6 months refrigerated, up to 1 year frozen

Pecans, a member of the hickory nut family, are rich, sweet, and extremely high in fat. The shells are easier to crack than those of hickory nuts, and the flavor of the nutmeat is slightly sweeter. Pecans keep best in the shell, so it is best to buy them that way. They are grown throughout the southern parts of the United States. Pecans can be expensive in stores. At your farmers' market, you will find better quality and prices. Toasting pecans in the oven before using is a good way of bringing out their flavor. Because of their high fat content, always check for rancidity before using.

Major vitamin and mineral content: A, C

Look for: sweet aroma; skin that gives slightly; smooth golden skin with purple streaks; no bruises; no green

Refrigerate: Yes.

Freeze: No.

Shelf life: 5 days refrigerated

The pepino is a small exotic member of the melon family. It originated in Peru and is now being grown in small quantities in California and Florida. The golden flesh is juicy and sweet. Pepinos are best eaten out of hand. Be sure to peel them.

*P*eppers, sweet (bell peppers)

Major vitamin and mineral content: A, potassium

Look for: firm, shiny peppers; hard skin

Refrigerate: Yes.

Freeze: Yes. Blanch and store in an airtight container.

Shelf life: about 5 days refrigerated, 6 months frozen

Bell peppers come in many colors—from the familiar green bell to the purplish-brown chocolate pepper—but one thing they have in common is extreme crunchiness and no heat (unlike chile peppers). Use them liberally in salads; stuff them with rice, meat, or tofu and bake; pickle them; or just cut 'em up and eat out of hand with some hummus or other dip. They make a great stir-fry with other vegetables.

See recipes on pages 133, 148, 174, and 181.

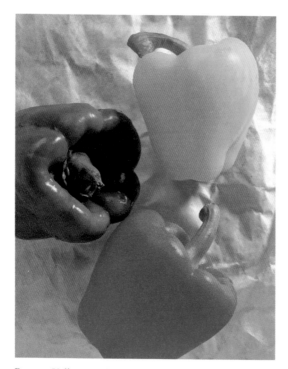

Pepper: Yellow, Red, Green

Major vitamin and mineral content: A, potassium

Look for: smooth skin, and bright orange color; Fuyu type should be firm and round, Hachiya should be soft but not mushy.

Refrigerate: Yes, but ripen at room temperature first.

Freeze: Yes. Freeze whole in airtight containers.

Shelf life: 4 days refrigerated, about 3 months frozen

The persimmon is a beautiful, sweet fruit that is a harbinger of autumn at farmers' markets in the regions where it is grown. This Japanese native has been grown in North America since the mid-nineteenth century and is slowly gaining a well-deserved place in the array of fall fruits. There are two types of persimmons you will find at the market. The Hachiya is the most common. It is oblong with a slightly pointed end. Do not eat it when it is hard—it is loaded with tannic acid and you'll be puckering up from now until doomsday. The tannic acid dissipates as the fruit ripens. It is ready to be eaten when it is very soft. By then, it is tangy and sweet, with a lovely custard-like texture. Fuyu persimmons are gaining in popularity and are appearing in greater numbers at farmers' markets. They are smaller and rounder than Hachiyas, and should be eaten while they are hard. Fuyus are best eaten out of hand, skin and all, or sliced and tossed into salads. Hachiyas lend themselves to puddings and other desserts, but they are also wonderful just plain. Scoop out the flesh and eat like custard.

*P*ine nut

Major vitamin and mineral content: potassium

Look for: no rancid smell

Refrigerate: Yes. Store in an airtight container.

Freeze: Yes. Store in an airtight container.

Shelf life: about 3 months refrigerated, 9 months in the freezer

Pine nuts, also known as pignoli and piñons, are the kernels of the pine cones of several varieties of pine tree. Each pine cone must be heated to extract even just one kernel, a labor-intensive process that is the reason why they are usually expensive. Piñons are harvested in the American Southwest. Pine nuts are roasted for snacks, and are a key ingredient in classic pesto. Because of their high fat content, pine nuts spoil easily, so it is important to store them in the refrigerator or freezer.

See recipe on page 139.

ineapple

Major vitamin and mineral content: A, C

Look for: firm skin; sweet aroma; red or orange color at the base; no fermented smell

Refrigerate: Not recommended. Stand the fruit upside down and let ripen at room temperature.

Freeze: No.

Shelf life: about 3 days at room temperature

Pineapple

The pineapples we eat in North America are usually flown in from Hawaii, but pineapples are now being grown in very small quantities in Florida and southern California. If you live in Hawaii or these areas, try to find freshly picked pineapple at your farmers' market. Even if it's expensive, it is an exquisite treat.

See recipe on page 181.

Pistachio

Major vitamin and mineral content: A, calcium, iron, phosphorus, thiamine

Look for: if unshelled, shells should be partly open.

Refrigerate: No.

Freeze: Yes, in an airtight container.

Shelf life: 3 months in an airtight container at room temperature, up to 1 year in the freezer

 Pistachios are widely cultivated in California and are a common sight at farmers' markets year-round. These nuts are sold shelled or unshelled. Some are raw, some are salted, some are flavored with garlic—they are all addictive snacks. Buy pistachios in their shells. They will taste fresher than the shelled nuts, which can become stale.

Plum

Major vitamin and mineral content: A, potassium

Look for: plump, firm fruit that gives slightly to pressure; bright color; unblemished skin

Refrigerate: Yes, but first ripen at room temperature.

Freeze: Yes. Slice and freeze in an airtight container.

Shelf life: about 5 days refrigerated, 6 months in the freezer

Plums: (top: Red; bottom: Black Amber)

Plums, succulent and sweet, originated in China about two thousand years ago. Luther Burbank studied plums from Japan in the 1880s and began to cultivate them. Today, plum varieties that Burbank developed in Santa Rosa, California, are grown all over the world. You will most likely find several varieties at your market, many descended from Burbank's hybrids. You will also find plums that are unique to your area. Plums range from the brilliant green Kelsey to the deep purple, almost black Black Friar. French plums, or prunes, are smaller than most varieties of plums and are almond-shaped. They are usually dried to makes prunes, but fresh ones can be found at your farmers' market. They make excellent tarts and cakes. Most plums are best eaten out of hand or made into preserves.

See recipe on page 184.

Major vitamin and mineral content: C, potassium

Look for: fruit that is heavy for its size; bright red color; no blemishes

Refrigerate: Yes.

Freeze: Yes. Seeds and juice can be frozen.

Shelf life: up to 2 months in the refrigerator

  The pomegranate is a symbol of fertility in many cultures. Its hard, leathery red skin encloses hundred of edible seeds, each one surrounded by sweet-tart translucent red pulp (these individual juice sacs are called arils). It is a difficult fruit to consume. To eat, cut the fruit in half and pry out the seeds; be sure to remove the white membrane. You can eat the seeds out of hand, make pomegranate juice, or use the seeds in sweet or savory sauces. Some growers sell pomegranate juice at their stands in addition to the fruit. If you are a pomegranate juice fan, this is good news. Pomegranate juice is delicious, but it takes forever to make.

Pomelo

Major vitamin and mineral content: C, potassium

Look for: aromatic fruit that is heavy for its size; smooth skin

Refrigerate: Yes.

Freeze: The juice can be frozen.

Shelf life: about 5 days refrigerated

The pomelo also goes by the name of Shaddock and Chinese grapefruit. Many believe it is the ancestor of the common grapefruit. It is grown extensively in Indochina, China, and Japan, and is now being cultivated in North America in citrus-growing areas. It is very much like a large grapefruit. The pulp, which is not as juicy as a grapefruit's, can be very sweet or tart. It can be used in the same way grapefruit is used. The rind, with the pith, is wonderful candied or preserved.

104

Major vitamin and mineral content: B_6, C, potassium

Look for: firm, well-shaped potatoes; no green tinge; no blemishes; no sprouts, wrinkles, or cracks

Refrigerate: No.

Freeze: No.

Shelf life: new potatoes, about 5 days; all others 2 to 4 weeks stored in a cool, dark, dry place, away from onions

    The humble potato has taken a giant step in our collective palate over the past few years, and there is no better place to witness this revolution than at your farmers' market. Gone are the days of just one or two kinds of potatoes. There are literally dozens of varieties of this New World native, each with its

Potatoes: (clockwise from top left: Baby Russetts; Blues; Idaho)

own unique consistency, taste, and color. Want to make a psychedelic potato salad? Use purple Peruvian new potatoes instead of red new potatoes. New potatoes are simply young potatoes of any variety; less of their sugar has been converted to starch, so they tend to hold their shape even after cooking. Charm your spuds-loving friends with mashed Red Bliss potatoes. Some of the other varieties you'll find are round white and red (great for mashed potatoes), russet (use for French fries), fingerlings, creamers, Yellow Finn, and Yukon Gold. There are many, many more. Experiment with unfamiliar potatoes. Never refrigerate them, though.

See recipes on pages 134, 137, 159, 162, and 164.

Major vitamin and mineral content: C, potassium; good source of dietary fiber

Look for: large, firm fruit; yellow color; sweet, musky aroma

Refrigerate: Yes.

Freeze: No.

Shelf life: up to 2 months refrigerated

The quince is an autumn fruit that grows all over North America. It tastes somewhat like a combination of apples and pears. It is quite tart and must be cooked rather than eaten raw. It is loaded with pectin, which makes it the ideal fruit for wonderful jams and preserves. It can be used in lamb dishes and in savory sauces for poultry and game, as well as in candies and desserts.

Major vitamin and mineral content: calcium, potassium

Look for: firm roots; good color for its variety

Refrigerate: Yes.

Freeze: No.

Shelf life: about 1 week refrigerated

Radishes

 This root vegetable is a member of the mustard family. Its flavor is peppery and refreshing. There are many varieties of radish to be found at your farmers' market, the most common being the round red ones we've all seen used as garnish. Try a daikon (Chinese radish) for a change. It is a huge long white radish with a flavor slightly less piquant than the common red one. Radishes are great snacks, just wash and eat. You can toss them into salads. Cooked and pureed radishes combined with cooked pureed carrots makes a nice side dish.

See recipe on page 160.

Rhubarb

Major vitamin and mineral content: A

Look for: crisp, medium stalks; bright color

Refrigerate: Yes.

Freeze: No.

Shelf life: up to 1 week refrigerated

Rhubarb

 Rhubarb, although used to make desserts, is actually a vegetable. It looks like red celery, but, unlike celery, it is extremely tart and should never be eaten raw. Rhubarb leaves contain toxic oxalic acid; if you buy rhubarb with the leaves still attached, discard them immediately. With all of these precautions, why bother with rhubarb? If it is sweetened and cooked properly, it is wonderful. Strawberry-rhubarb pie is an American classic. Look for field-grown rhubarb as opposed to hothouse-grown—field-grown has more flavor and better color.

See recipe on page 189.

*R*utabaga

Major vitamin and mineral content: A, C, potassium

Look for: smooth, firm, pale yellow roots; roots that are heavy for their size; purplish tops

Refrigerate: Yes.

Freeze: No.

Shelf life: up to 2 months refrigerated

 Rutabagas are a sweetish root vegetable that is thought to be a cross between a cabbage and a turnip. They can be cooked like potatoes and have a hearty flavor. Use them in winter soups and stews.

Salad greens

Major vitamin and mineral content: A, C, calcium, iron, potassium

Look for: fresh, crisp leaves; no soft spots or blemishes

Refrigerate: Yes.

Freeze: No.

Shelf life: depending on variety, up to 5 days refrigerated

Salad greens: (clockwise from top left: French Crisp, Red Leaf, Romaine, Green Leaf, Mizuna, Lolla Rossa, Ruby Red)

CHICHAKO RANCH,
British Columbia

*S*hirley Dalke was born in Davis, California, but her family moved to Canada when she was still a young girl. She grew up in Vancouver, British Columbia.

Like many Vancouverites, Shirley and her husband worked in the burgeoning film and television industries of Vancouver. Shirley was a successful cameraperson until an on-the-job accident left her unable to lift and operate heavy camera equipment. Her film career was over, and she was exhausted—emotionally, mentally, and physically. After much soul-searching, Shirley and her husband decided to leave Vancouver for the quieter town of Gibsons, on the "sunshine coast" of western British Columbia. They bought a house and five acres of land, and Shirley's days as a farmer began on Chichako Ranch.

Shirley is an organic farmer. She uses no chemical fertilizers or pesticides, and her soil has been analyzed for chemical residue (none there). Her methods, and a diversified crop, are best for healthy soil, keeping it full of nutrients and beneficial bacteria.

Shirley specializes in a variety of hot peppers, lettuces, and cabbages. She cultivates over 1000 herb plants. In the spring, she grows snow peas and Nantes-type carrots. She also makes condiments from her crops, bottling wonderful hot sauces, salsas, jellies, and marinades. She and her husband also raise ducks, geese, and sheep, with some Border collies to keep the flock in line.

Shirley sells all of her products at the Granville Island Public Market in Vancouver. It is a lovely market, on an island under the Granville Street Bridge, a major bridge in the heart of the city. Farmers from all over western Canada bring fresh produce in during the week so all can come and sample the good life in Canada.

Shirley Dahlke
Chichako Ranch
RR #2, S-14, C-19
Gibsons, BC
V0N 1V0, Canada
604-886-7859

 There are hundreds of varieties of lettuce and other salad greens being grown, and you will find the widest assortment of them at your farmers' market. From spicy mizuna to soft-tasting butter lettuce, from elegant red radicchio to nutty mâche, or lamb's lettuce, the farmers' market affords you the pleasure of creating wonderful salads and sandwiches. Remember that the darker the leaf, the more nutrients are present. Many greens growers are now selling mesclun salad mix. This convenient mixture of fresh exotic lettuces and greens is washed, trimmed, and ready to serve. It may seem to cost more than buying heads of lettuce, but the work of cleaning and trimming has been done for you, and you need only buy what you need—there's no waste. Buying salad mix is a good way to have salad greens readily available in your kitchen. Greenhouse farming makes most of these greens available year-round.

See recipes on pages 144, 146, 149, and 150.

Snow Peas and Sugar Snap Peas

Major vitamin and mineral content: A, potassium

Look for: Snow peas: bright green, flat pods; no visible peas. Sugar snaps: bright green pods with green stem ends

Refrigerate: Yes.

Freeze: No.

Shelf life: 1 to 2 days refrigerated

Snow peas and sugar snaps are both valued for their edible pods. Crisp, tender, green, and sweet, they can be used in stir-fries and are wonderful steamed or sautéed as a side dish. Before cooking, the stems should be removed. Both kinds cook very quickly—be careful not to overcook them.

See recipes on pages 168 and 174.

Sorrel

Major vitamin and mineral content: A, C, calcium, phosphorous, potassium, magnesium

Look for: bright green, crisp leaves; no woody stems or yellowed, wilting leaves

Refrigerate: Yes.

Freeze: No.

Shelf life: about 4 days refrigerated

Sorrel is actually an herb, but it is used somewhat differently from other herbs. It has a very strong taste because it contains oxalic acid, like spinach and rhubarb. It should be cooked in glass or stainless steel pans only, as it will react with other materials. This bitter herb is wonderful in cream of sorrel soup or baked into an herb bread. The first sorrel of the spring is especially tender and less acidic, so it can be used, sparingly, in salads or cooked as a vegetable.

Spinach

Major vitamin and mineral content: A, C, calcium, iron, good source of dietary fiber

Look for: Crisp, deep green leaves; no wilting

Refrigerate: Yes.

Freeze: No.

Shelf life: 3 days refrigerated

Spinach, the vegetable of champions, is also one of the most delicious of the green leafy family. It originated in the Middle East, and has been feeding humans for centuries. The Spanish were the first to bring spinach to North America. Spinach is an extremely versatile vegetable. It is wonderful raw in salads, makes great soups, is a terrific side dish, adds a unique flavor to ordinary humus, and of course, is the key ingredient in any dish prepared a la Florentine. It contains some oxalic acid, which inhibits the body's abili-

Spinach

ty to absorb calcium and iron, but it is a nutritious vegetable nonetheless. Spinach. like many other greens, should be washed thoroughly, since it can be very sandy and gritty.

See recipe on page 152 and 186.

Sprouts

Major vitamin and mineral content: B, C, E, potassium; source of dietary fiber

Look for: plump, fresh-smelling sprouts; no bruises, brown spots, or slime

Refrigerate: Yes.

Freeze: No.

Shelf life: 2 to 3 days refrigerated

 Edible sprouts, germinated beans or seeds, are becoming more popular as we become more concerned with what we eat. They are good and good for you! Alfalfa, radish, mung bean, clover, sunflower, soybean sprouts, and more can all be found at your farmers' market. It is best to buy them there, because they are tastiest and most nutritious when they are absolutely fresh. No food is more associated with "health food" than sprouts. Once you get past the idea

Sprouts: (clockwise from bottom right: Alfalfa; Dicer, Sunflower, Buckwheat, Radish, center: Pea)

that they taste like grass—they don't—you can enhance your sandwiches or salads with a heap of fresh sprouts. Try mixing pungent radish sprouts with sweet alfalfa and clover sprouts. Use mung bean sprouts in a stir-fry. They are all practically no-calorie foods and are packed with nutrients.

See recipe on page 140 and 151.

Squash, Summer

Major vitamin and mineral content: A, C, niacin

Look for: small squash; bright colors; no spots or bruises

Refrigerate: Yes.

Freeze: No.

Shelf life: up to 5 days refrigerated

The summer squashes—zucchini, yellow crook-neck, pattypan, and straight-neck—are picked when they are immature, so their skin is still tender and the entire squash is edible. Buy the smaller squash; the larger the vegetable, the more fibrous and less sweet it will be. All

Zucchini

of the summer squashes are enormously popular and are grown everywhere. They are a popular home garden vegetable because they thrive under almost any conditions. Look for unusual varieties at your farmers' market.

See recipes on pages 164 and 168.

*S*quash, Winter

Major vitamin and mineral content: A, C, beta carotene, iron, potassium, riboflavin

Look for: hard shells; no pitting or soft spots; squash with stems; squash that is heavy for its size

Refrigerate: No.

Freeze: Cooked puree can be frozen.

Shelf life: 3 to 4 weeks (or longer) in a cool, dark place

Winter squashes include the buttercup, Cuban squash, delicata, golden nugget, kabocha, sweet dumpling, acorn, butternut, Hubbard, spaghetti, turban, and pumpkin. There are hundreds of varieties,

Squash: (clockwise from top right: Acorn, Pattypan, Kabocha, Butternut, Spaghetti)

but these are the ones you will most likely find at your farmers' market. Most winter squashes have a thick, hard skin. You may even need a cleaver and mallet to open some of the harder-skinned varieties. Winter squash can be baked, steamed, pureed, even stir-fried. The spaghetti squash, so-called because its pulp is composed of long translucent threads, can be served with sauces in the same way you would serve pasta. Hubbard squash pulp can be used in place of pumpkin for unusual but equally delicious pies and breads. Pumpkin-stuffed tortellini or ravioli is wonderful. Winter squash seeds can be roasted and eaten as snacks.

See recipes on pages 158, 162, and 199.

Major vitamin and mineral content: A, C, calcium, iron

Look for: fresh looking blossoms; closed buds; soft and limp is OK

Refrigerate: Yes.

Freeze: No.

Shelf life: 1 day refrigerated

Squash blossoms are the flowers of summer squash. The most popular and available kind come from zucchini. These yellowish-orange flowers are delicious, delicately flavored and slightly reminiscent of the squash from whence they came. Use them as a garnish, or add to salads. A good way to prepare them is to batter dip and fry them. They are also delicious stuffed with a soft, aromatic cheese.

See recipe on page 177.

Zucchini Blossoms

117

Major vitamin and mineral content: A, C, K, calcium

Look for: firm, uniformly red berries (size doesn't matter); no green or white areas

Refrigerate: Yes. Do not wash or hull until ready to eat.

Freeze: Yes. Freeze whole unwashed berries in airtight plastic bags or containers.

Shelf life: 1 to 3 days in the refrigerator

Strawberries are the first berries of the summer season and may begin to appear in farmers' markets as early as late April, depending on where you live. They are very fragile and deteriorate rapidly, so local markets are your best bet for freshness and flavor. Strawberries come in several varieties, but there is no reason to seek out a specific type. Buy from local growers; the best strawberries are the ones that are grown nearby. They simply taste better than supermarket berries that have been shipped across the country. Strawberries will not ripen once they have been picked, so buy them fully ripe and red. If you live in California or Florida, you will probably be able to buy locally grown berries year-round. If you don't live in these states, keep in mind that the farther a strawberry has to travel, the less flavorful it will be. Strawberries are extremely versatile. When you find strawberries that you like, stock up and freeze or can them. You can use them in all kinds of recipes throughout the year. They are scrumptious in tarts, jams, ice cream, and salsa. If you find a farmer who sells wild strawberries, just eat them out of hand.

See recipes on pages 143, 151, and 190.

Major vitamin and mineral content: A, C, beta carotene

Look for: firm potatoes; no bruises or soft spots; small to medium in size

Refrigerate: No.

Freeze: No.

Shelf life: up to 4 weeks in a cool, dark, dry place

Sweet Potatoes

 Sweet potatoes are edible roots that are in no way related to YAMS. If you see a sweet potato that is about the size of a football, you are looking at a yam. (If you see a yam that is about the size of a baseball or smaller, you are looking at a sweet potato.) The harvest begins early in the fall, and by Thanksgiving, we are awash in sweet orange-fleshed ones, red sweets with yellow flesh, and white sweets with pale flesh. Darker varieties tend to be sweeter. You can use sweet potatoes anywhere you would use a regular potato. Try making French fries with them. Or make a sweet potato pie for the holidays. Sweet potato chips are even more addicting than regular chips.

See recipes on pages 138 and 170.

Major vitamin and mineral content: A, C

Look for: firm fruit that is heavy for its size; no blemishes; rich color (yellow fruit is sweeter than red)

Refrigerate: Yes, but first ripen at room temperature.

Freeze: No.

Shelf life: about 10 days refrigerated

Tamarillos, also known as tree tomatoes, originated in New Zealand but now are being grown in North America in small quantities. Their appearance may remind you of tomatoes, but they are actually related to the eggplant. They resemble neither in flavor. Tamarillos are full of flavor, but they can be tart. Some can be eaten out of hand, peeled, but they usually need some sugar added to bring out their flavor and cut the tartness. Tamarillos are wonderful in chutney and relishes.

Taro root

Major vitamin and mineral content: C, iron, potassium; good source of dietary fiber

Look for: firm roots; smooth skin

Refrigerate: Yes.

Freeze: No.

Shelf life: up to 4 days in the refrigerator

Taro root, also known as dasheen, is an edible tuber. It is an essential ingredient in many Asian, Caribbean, African, and Latin American dishes and is perhaps best known as the ingredient in the Hawaiian dish poi. It grows in the tropics, but it is also cultivated in the southern United States. It tastes like a combination of potato and chestnut. It can be used as a flavorful thickener for stews and soups. Add it to stir-fries. Deep-fried taro chips are as good as, if not better than, French fries. Taro must be fully cooked before it is eaten.

120

Tomatillo

Major vitamin and mineral content: A, C

Look for: firm fruit; dry, tight husks

Refrigerate: Yes.

Freeze: No.

Shelf life: up to 1 month refrigerated

The tomatillo, or Mexican green tomato, is popping up at more markets throughout North America. Many pepper growers are growing tomatillos in response to our increasingly sophisticated national palate. Tomatillos are small green cousins of tomatoes. Like the **cape gooseberry**, they come wrapped in their own little paper husks. They are best when cooked—toss some into your marinara sauce for a Mexican touch— but they also make great contributions to salsas and guacamole in their raw form.

See recipe on page 187.

Tomatillos

Tomatoes: (top: Dutch Hothouse; middle: Yellow Cherry; bottom left: Yellow; bottom right: Pear)

Tomato

Major vitamin and mineral content: A, B, C, iron, phosphorous, potassium

Look for: firm fruit that is heavy for its size; no ridges at the stem area; firm but with a slight give; rich color

Refrigerate: Never.

Freeze: Yes, cut-up or pureed.

Shelf life: depending on the variety, 2 to 7 days at room temperature

You may think that tomatoes are available year-round at your supermarket, but you are wrong. Those pale pink things in the produce section in January are a poor substitute for the greatest summer vegetable (it's really a fruit) of all—the tomato! And what a tomato! Beefsteaks are great, but at your farmers' market you will find vine-ripened yellow and pink Marvel Stripes, tiny red Sweet 100s, cherry tomatoes, yellow pear tomatoes, green-striped Zebra tomatoes, burgundy Brandywines,

122

orange tomatoes, Romas—the list is literally endless. Many growers are experimenting with antique breeds of tomatoes. These nonhybrids, such as the Marvel Stripe, are delicious but more perishable than regular store-bought tomatoes. The only place to find them is at the farmers' market. You cannot imagine the taste difference between a vine-ripened tomato and a store-bought one. There is no contest. Once you've had a farmers' market fresh vine-ripened tomato, you'll never go back to the waxy supermarket variety again—and you'll count the days until local tomatoes appear on your favorite grower's table again.

See recipes on pages 128, 130, 136, 142, and 166.

Turnip

Major vitamin and mineral content: C

Look for: small turnips that are firm and heavy for their size; bright and fresh-looking greens

Refrigerate: Yes.

Freeze: No.

Shelf life: up to 4 weeks refrigerated

 The turnip is a popular sweet and delicately flavored root vegetable that can be used in stews and soups, much like **potatoes** or **rutabagas**. The greens are also edible, and quite good. (See **greens**.) Treat a turnip as you would any root vegetable: Steam it, mash it, puree it. With a dab of butter, it is wonderful.

See recipe on page 167.

Ugli fruit

Major vitamin and mineral content: C

Look for: Fruit should be heavy for its size; thick, yellow-green skin

Refrigerate: Yes.

Freeze: No.

Shelf life: 1 week at room temperature; up to 3 weeks refrigerated

Ugli Fruit

 This large, unusual member of the citrus family is available on a very limited basis in the most tropical areas of North America. It is a citrus fruit with a very high vitamin C content. Your citrus grower may sell them at the farmers' market when they are in season, and they are worth sampling. The taste is somewhat like a combination of a grapefruit and an orange, although some people detect hints of tangerine in an ugli fruit. Use ugli fruit in any way you would use a grapefruit. Just cut it in half and enjoy.

Walnut

Major vitamin and mineral content: potassium

Look for: shells without holes or cracks; nuts in the shell should not rattle when shaken; shelled nutmeats should be plump and crisp

Refrigerate: Yes.

Freeze: Yes.

Shelf life: up to 6 months refrigerated, 1 year frozen

Walnuts, both English and black varieties, are the most popular nuts for cooking, especially baking. They are available year-round. Many people love to eat them out of hand. They are versatile and can be used in savory dishes as well as desserts.

See recipe on page 141.

Watermelon

Major vitamin and mineral content: A, C

Look for: symmetrical shape, with no flat sides; melons that sound hollow when lightly thumped; dull-colored skin

Refrigerate: Yes, but only once cut.

Freeze: No.

Shelf life: whole melons, about 10 days at room temperature; cut melon, refrigerated and tightly wrapped in plastic, about 1 week

Watermelon comes in many shapes, sizes, and colors. This refreshing melon comes originally from Africa. It is over 90 percent water. It can be oblong or round, and its flesh can be red, white, or yellow. It can weigh as little as five pounds or as much as thirty-five. It may be seedless or with seeds. Whatever type you choose, chances are it will be sugar-sweet and delicious. All parts of the watermelon can be eaten. The seeds can be roasted for snacks, the rind can be made into watermelon pickle, and, of course, the flesh can be eaten out of hand on a hot summer's day. Watermelon can be juiced, or it can be cut into cubes or balls for fruit salad. Watermelons grow all over North America. Some of the varieties you may find at your farmers' market are Jubilee, Charleston Gray, Golden Doll, Crimson Sweet, Sangria, and Sugar Baby. There are countless more—taste and find your favorite.

Watermelon

Major vitamin and mineral content: A, C

Look for: tight, smooth skin; no blemishes

Refrigerate: No.

Freeze: No.

Shelf life: up to 4 weeks in a cool, dry place

The yam is not a **sweet potato**. It is unlikely that you will find this tuber at your market. It is still grown mostly in the tropics, and the North American market has not yet warranted farming up here. Yams are listed here because you will often see sweet potatoes mislabeled as yams. Whether they're called garnet or jewel yams, if they're grown in the United States or Canada, they are sweet potatoes. End of story.

Recipes

Note: The ingredients that appear in **boldface** throughout the recipes have a corresponding entry in the preceding ingredients section.

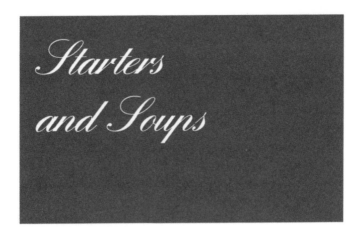

Asparagus with Tomato-Basil Coulis

SERVES 4

½ cup plus 1 tablespoon olive oil
10 cloves garlic, minced
4 **shallots,** minced
3 **tomatoes,** peeled and quartered
¾ cup vegetable juice (V8)
2 tablespoons chopped fresh **basil**
1 tablespoon chopped fresh flat-leaf parsley
Salt and freshly ground pepper to taste
1 cup dry white wine
2 tablespoons unsalted butter
1½ pounds **asparagus,** blanched in boiling salted water until
  crisp-tender

GARNISH

2 **tomatoes,** peeled and cut into small dice
Chives, cut into 1-inch lengths
Minced scallions
Fresh **basil** leaves

1 In a medium sauté pan, heat 1 tablespoon of the oil
over medium heat. Add the garlic and shallots and sauté
until soft, about 2 minutes. Add the tomatoes, vegetable
juice, basil, and parsley, season with salt and pepper, and
cook until heated through, 5 to 7 minutes.

2 Pour the mixture into a food processor or blender.
Pour the wine into the pan and heat over medium heat,

128

stirring to release any cooked juices from the bottom of the pan. Add to the tomato mixture and puree. With the motor running, add the remaining ½ cup oil in a slow, steady stream and process for 2 minutes.

3 In a large sauté pan, melt the butter. Add the asparagus and sauté until crisp-tender, 4 to 5 minutes.

4 To serve, cover the bottom of 4 plates with the coulis. Arrange the asparagus in a fan over the coulis on each plate. Arrange the diced tomatoes at the base of the asparagus fans. Garnish with chives, scallions, and basil leaves.

$\mathcal{B}$aby Artichokes with Lemon-Parmesan Dressing

SERVES 4

4 cloves garlic
1 small serrano **chile,** halved
1 bay leaf
1 **lemon,** halved
Salt and freshly ground pepper
16 baby **artichokes,** bottoms trimmed and tough outer leaves removed
¼ cup extra-virgin olive oil
2 tablespoons cider vinegar
1 tablespoon chopped fresh flat-leaf parsley
1 **shallot,** finely chopped
2 tablespoons freshly grated Parmesan cheese

1 In a heavy stainless steel saucepan, bring 8 cups of water to a boil. Add the garlic, chile, bay leaf, lemon, and a pinch each of salt and pepper. Drop in the artichokes, reduce the heat, and simmer until tender, 8 to 12 minutes. Remove from the heat and let cool in the cooking liquid while you prepare the dressing.

2 In a medium bowl, whisk together the oil, vinegar, parsley, and shallot. Whisk in the parmesan. Season with salt and pepper to taste.

3 Drain the artichokes and gently squeeze each one to remove excess water. Quarter the artichokes, add to the dressing, and toss well. Serve immediately.

$\mathscr{C}$eviche of Sea Bass with Roasted Corn and Tomatoes

SERVES 4

Three 6- to 8-ounce sea bass fillets, skin removed, cut into
   3- by $1/2$-inch strips
1 cup fresh lime juice
$1/2$ cup fresh orange juice
$1/2$ cup fresh lemon juice
$1/2$ cup thinly sliced red onion
2 teaspoons minced **jalapeños**
2 ears **corn** in the husk
1 cup olive oil
6 plum **tomatoes,** seeded and cut into $1/4$-inch-thick strips
$1/2$ cup slivered fresh **cilantro**
2 teaspoons salt
1 teaspoon white pepper

1 Preheat the oven to 375 degrees F.

2 In a medium bowl, combine the bass, lime, orange, and lemon juices, red onion, and jalapeños. Cover and refrigerate for 6 hours.

3 Meanwhile, roast the corn: Pull the corn husks away from the cobs, remove the silk, and take off all but one layer of husks. Push the husks back around the cobs. Soak the ears in a large bowl filled with cold water for 10 minutes, until slightly soft. Place on a baking sheet and roast the ears for about 20 minutes, until tender. Let cool. Scrape the kernels off the cobs and set aside.

4 Just before serving, drain off half of the marinating liquid from the ceviche and discard. Add the oil, corn, tomatoes, and cilantro to the ceviche and toss well. Season with the salt and white pepper. Serve chilled.

Garlic Toasts with Roma Sauce

ROMA SAUCE

½ large **red onion,** cut into 4 pieces
½ cup lightly packed fresh **basil** leaves
1 pound ripe **plum tomatoes,** halved and seeded
3 tablespoons freshly grated Parmesan
3 tablespoons fresh lime juice
2 tablespoons olive oil
1 tablespoon balsamic vinegar

GARLIC BUTTER

2 large **garlic** cloves
1 large shallot
8 tablespoons (1 stick) unsalted butter, at room temperature
Salt and freshly ground pepper to taste

Sixteen ½-inch-thick slices baguette (French bread)

1 To make the sauce, in a food processor, puree the onion, basil leaves, tomatoes, parmesan cheese, and lime juice. Add the oil and vinegar and process until thick and smooth.

2 To make the garlic butter, in a food processor, finely chop the garlic and shallot. Add the butter and process until smooth. Season with salt and pepper.

3 To make the toasts, preheat the broiler. Arrange the bread slices on a baking sheet. Spread with the garlic butter. Broil until brown and crisp.

4 Pour the sauce into a small bowl for dipping. Arrange the garlic toast and the bowl of sauce on a platter and serve.

ravlax

SERVES 8 TO 10

3 pounds very fresh center-cut **salmon** fillet, in one piece
2 large bunches **dill**
1/4 cup kosher salt
1/4 cup sugar
2 tablespoons crushed white peppercorns

1 Cut the salmon fillet in half. Place one half skin side down in a deep glass dish. Spread the dill over the fish. Sprinkle the salt, sugar, and peppercorns over the dill. Top with the other piece of fish, skin side up. Cover the salmon with foil. Place a board (or a small cutting board) on top and place a 5-pound weight on top of it. Refrigerate for at least 2 days or up to 3, turning the salmon every 12 hours and basting with the accumulated juices.

2 To serve, remove the fish from the marinade. Scrape off the dill and spices and pat dry with paper towels. Slice thinly on the diagonal and serve.

erbed Goat Cheese

SERVES 4 TO 6

One 11-ounce log **Montrachet,** cut into 4 pieces
1/4 cup heavy cream
3 bunches **chives,** finely chopped
1 teaspoon dried thyme
1 teaspoon grated lemon zest
1/2 teaspoon fresh lemon juice
1/2 teaspoon freshly ground pepper

1 Place the Montrachet in a food processor. With the motor running, slowly add the cream and process until smooth. Scrape into a bowl.

2 Whisk in the chives, thyme, lemon zest and juice, and pepper. Cover and refrigerate for at least 2 hours to allow the flavors to blend.

3 Transfer the cheese to a serving bowl and serve with crusty bread.

Roasted Eggplant and Pepper Salad with Pita Bread

SERVES 4

1 medium **eggplant** (about 1¼ pounds), cut into ½-inch cubes
1 large **green bell pepper,** cored, seeded, and cut into ½-inch-wide strips
1 large **red bell pepper,** cored, seeded, and cut into ½-inch-wide strips
4 large cloves garlic (unpeeled)
¼ cup olive oil
¾ cup red wine vinegar
1 tablespoon ground cumin
Salt and freshly ground pepper to taste
4 warm pita breads, cut into wedges

1 Preheat the oven to 450 degrees F. Spray a baking sheet with nonstick cooking spray.

2 Combine the eggplant, bell peppers, and garlic in a large bowl. Add the oil and toss well. Spread the vegetables on the prepared baking sheet.

3 Bake, stirring frequently, for about 50 minutes, until the eggplant is browned and all the vegetables are tender.

4 Remove the garlic and reserve. Scrape the vegetables and pan juices into a large bowl.

5 Peel the roasted garlic. Combine the vinegar, cumin, and salt and pepper in a food processor, add the garlic and puree.

6 Add the garlic dressing to the vegetable mixture and toss well. Let cool, tossing occasionally.

7 Serve with the pita bread.

Roasted Haricots Verts with Potatoes and Fennel

SERVES 4

2 **fennel** bulbs, trimmed and quartered lengthwise
1½ pounds small **red new potatoes,** thinly sliced
2/3 cup olive oil
1 teaspoon kosher salt
1½ pounds **haricots verts**
Freshly ground pepper to taste

1 Preheat the oven to 425 degrees F.

2 Combine the fennel, potatoes, and oil in a large bowl and toss well. Spread the vegetables on a baking sheet and sprinkle with the salt. Roast for 30 minutes.

3 Add the beans to the vegetables, toss well, and roast until the beans are lightly browned, 10 to 15 minutes longer. Season with the pepper, and serve hot or at room temperature.

Spiced Almonds

2 CUPS

½ teaspoon ground cumin
½ teaspoon chili powder
½ teaspoon curry powder
½ teaspoon garlic powder
½ teaspoon cayenne pepper
¼ teaspoon ground ginger
¼ teaspoon ground cinnamon
2 tablespoons olive oil
2 cups unblanched whole **almonds**
1 tablespoon kosher salt

1 Preheat the oven to 325 degrees F.

2 In a small bowl, mix the cumin, chili powder, curry powder, garlic, cayenne, ginger, and cinnamon together.

3 Heat the oil in a nonstick sauté pan over low heat. Add the spice mixture and cook, stirring constantly, until fragrant, 3 to 4 minutes. Remove from the heat.

Salads and Side Dishes

Arugula and Pine Nut Salad

SERVES 4

⅓ cup **pine nuts**
4 ounces **arugula** (1 large bunch)
4 **scallions,** thinly sliced
2 thin slices prosciutto, cut into thin strips
8 sprigs **chervil,** coarsely chopped

DRESSING

3 tablespoons extra-virgin olive oil
1 tablespoon walnut oil
½ teaspoon Dijon mustard
Juice of 1 **lemon**
Salt and freshly ground pepper to taste

1 In a small saucepan, toast the pine nuts over medium-high heat, stirring constantly, until golden brown, about 3 minutes. Transfer to a plate and let cool.

2 Place the arugula, scallions, prosciutto, and chervil in a serving bowl. Toss gently to mix.

3 To make the dressing, in a small bowl, whisk all the ingredients together. Pour over the salad and toss. Sprinkle with the pine nuts.

$\mathcal{B}$ean Sprout, Cucumber, and Crab Salad

SERVES 4

12 ounces fresh **bean sprouts,** rinsed and picked through
1 small **cucumber**
1 cup crabmeat, picked over for shells and cartilage
3 tablespoons rice vinegar
3 tablespoons light soy sauce
Generous pinch of salt
1/2 cup sunflower oil
Freshly ground pepper to taste

1 In a large pot of boiling water, blanch the bean sprouts for about 2 minutes. Drain and let cool.

2 Trim the ends of the cucumber and cut it in half. Slice off the skin and underlying flesh in 1/4-inch-thick slices, avoiding the seedy center. Julienne the peelings and place in a large bowl of ice water. Drain well.

3 In a large bowl, combine the crabmeat, bean sprouts, and cucumber. Cover and chill for 1 to 1 1/2 hours.

4 In a small bowl, combine the vinegar, soy sauce, and salt. Using a small whisk, beat in the oil in a thin, steady stream. Season with pepper, pour over the salad, and toss well.

$\mathcal{B}$lack Bean and Corn Salad

SERVES 4

2 cups **corn** kernels (3 to 4 ears)
2 cups cooked **black beans**
1 large **tomato,** seeded and diced
3 **scallions,** thinly sliced
1 **jalapeño** pepper, seeded and diced
1/4 cup chopped fresh **cilantro**
1 tablespoon olive oil
1 tablespoon balsamic vinegar
1 tablespoon fresh lime juice
Salt and freshly ground pepper to taste

1 In a large pot of boiling water, cook the corn until just tender, about 3 minutes. Drain. When cool enough to handle, scrape the kernels from the cobs.

2 In a medium bowl, combine the beans, corn, tomato, scallions, jalapeño, and cilantro.

3 Combine the remaining ingredients in a small bowl and whisk well to combine. Add to the bean salad and toss well.

Carrot and Walnut Salad

SERVES 4

6 large **carrots,** shredded (about 3 cups)
2 tablespoons extra-virgin olive oil
1 tablespoon plus 1 teaspoon fresh lemon juice
1/2 teaspoon salt
3 tablespoons chopped **walnuts,** lightly toasted

1 In a medium bowl, toss the carrots with the oil. Add the remaining ingredients and toss well.

2 Serve at room temperature or chilled.

Cherry Tomato and Fresh Herb Salad

*C*herry Tomato and Fresh Herb Salad

SERVES 6

2 pints **cherry tomatoes,** halved
10 **scallions,** very thinly sliced
1/4 cup minced fresh flat-leaf **parsley**
1/4 cup minced fresh **basil**
1/4 cup minced fresh **mint**
1/2 cup rice vinegar
1/4 cup sunflower or other flavorless oil
2 tablespoons fresh orange juice
Pinch of sugar
Freshly ground pepper to taste

1 In a large bowl, toss together the tomatoes, scallions, and herbs.

2 In a small bowl, whisk together the vinegar, oil, orange juice, sugar, and pepper. Pour the dressing over the tomatoes and toss. Cover and let sit for 20 to 30 minutes before serving.

Orange and Onion Salad

SERVES 4

4 large **navel oranges**
2 tablespoons red wine vinegar
¼ cup extra-virgin olive oil
2 tablespoons fresh oregano leaves
1 small **red onion,** sliced into paper-thin rings
¼ cup Niçoise olives, pitted
¼ teaspoon chopped fresh **chives**
Freshly ground pepper

1 Peel and section the oranges. Place in a shallow serving dish and sprinkle with the vinegar, oil, and oregano. Toss, cover, and refrigerate for 30 minutes.

2 Toss the oranges again. Arrange on 4 plates with the sliced onions. Scatter the olives over the top and garnish with the chives and a grinding of pepper.

Roasted Red Pepper and Cucumber Salad

Roasted Red Pepper and Cucumber Salad

SERVES 4

2 medium **red bell peppers**
3 medium **cucumbers,** peeled, halved lengthwise, and seeded
¼ cup plus 2 tablespoons balsamic vinegar
3 tablespoons olive oil
Salt and freshly ground pepper to taste
2 to 3 shallots, minced
Chopped fresh flat-leaf parsley for garnish

1 Roast the peppers over a gas flame or under the broiler until charred on all sides. Place in a paper bag and let cool. Peel, core, seed, and slice the peppers into strips. Set aside.

2 Cut the cucumber halves crosswise in half and cut into strips about the same thickness as the pepper strips. Set aside.

3 Put the vinegar in a small bowl. Whisk in the oil, then whisk in the salt and pepper.

4 Put the shallots in a large bowl. Add the roasted peppers and the cucumbers. Add the vinaigrette and toss to coat. Adjust the seasoning if necessary, and sprinkle with parsley.

*S*autéed Pears with Mâche

SERVES 4

1 clove garlic, finely chopped
1 small **shallot,** finely chopped
2½ tablespoons sherry vinegar
1½ teaspoons Dijon mustard
1 teaspoon chopped fresh thyme
½ cup plus 2 tablespoons olive oil
Salt and freshly ground pepper to taste
3 medium ripe **Anjou pears,** peeled, halved, cored, and thinly sliced
4 cups **mâche leaves**

1 In a medium bowl, combine the garlic, shallot, vinegar, mustard, and thyme and whisk to blend. Gradually whisk in ½ cup of the oil. Season with salt and pepper. Cover and let stand at room temperature to allow the flavors to blend.

2 Heat the remaining 2 tablespoons olive oil in a large sauté pan. Add the pear slices and sauté for 4 to 5 minutes, or until soft.

3 Meanwhile, arrange the mâche on salad plates.

4 Place the pear slices over the mache and spoon some of the dressing over each salad. Serve.

Sautéed Radicchio and Endive with Garlic-Mustard Vinaigrette

SERVES 4

1/4 cup extra-virgin olive oil
2 tablespoons Champagne vinegar
4 cloves **garlic,** crushed
1/4 teaspoon dry mustard
1 medium head **radicchio,** washed, dried, and cut into 8 wedges
2 heads **Belgian endive,** washed, dried, and cut lengthwise into quarters
Salt and freshly ground pepper to taste

1 In a small bowl, combine the oil, vinegar, garlic, and dry mustard.

2 Place both lettuces in a large bowl. Sprinkle with salt and pepper and toss well. Pour the vinaigrette over the lettuces and toss thoroughly.

3 Heat a large heavy skillet until smoking hot. Add the radicchio and endive to the pan and toss rapidly for 20 to 30 seconds. Serve immediately.

Shrimp and Grape Salad

SERVES 4

1 pound medium shrimp, shelled and deveined
1/2 cup sour cream
1/2 cup mayonnaise
1 cup seedless **green grapes**
1/4 cup chopped fresh **dill**
Salt and freshly ground pepper to taste

1 Bring a large pot of salted water to a boil. Drop in the shrimp and cook for 1 minute only. Drain and let cool, then transfer to a bowl.

2 In a small bowl, whisk the sour cream and mayonnaise until smooth. Pour over the shrimp and toss gently. Add the grapes, dill, and salt and pepper and toss well. Cover and refrigerate for 4 hours.

3 Just before serving, toss the salad again. Adjust the seasoning if necessary.

Strawberry Salad

SERVES 4

2 tablespoons fresh lemon juice
1 tablespoon plus 1 teaspoon superfine sugar
¾ teaspoon almond extract
2 pints **strawberries,** rinsed, hulled, and halved
2 tablespoons slivered fresh **mint**
2 tablespoons julienne strips of **lemon** zest

1 In a large bowl, whisk together the lemon juice, sugar, and almond extract. Add the strawberries and toss. Cover and refrigerate for up to 2 hours.

2 Just before serving, gently stir in the mint and lemon zest.

Sweet-and-Sour Sprout Salad

SERVES 2 TO 4

¾ cup thinly sliced **white onions**
4 cups **mung bean sprouts**
1 **English cucumber,** peeled and thinly sliced
1 medium **carrot,** grated
½ cup water
3 tablespoons honey
3 tablespoons cider vinegar
3 tablespoons olive oil
1 teaspoon celery seeds
¼ teaspoon salt
Butter lettuce leaves for serving

1 Combine the onions, bean sprouts, cucumber, and carrot in a large bowl and toss.

2 In a small stainless steel saucepan, combine the water, honey, vinegar, oil, celery seeds, and salt and bring to a boil. Pour over the vegetables and toss well. Cover and refrigerate for at least 24 hours, or up to 3 days.

Warm Spinach and Basil Salad

SERVES 4

6 cups **spinach** leaves, rinsed and dried
2 cups fresh **basil** leaves
½ cup olive oil
3 cloves garlic, finely chopped
½ cup **pine nuts**
4 ounces prosciutto, diced
Salt and freshly ground pepper to taste
¾ cup freshly grated Parmesan cheese

1 In a large bowl, toss the spinach and basil together.

2 Heat the oil in a medium sauté pan over medium heat. Add the garlic and pine nuts and sauté until the nuts begin to brown lightly, 3 to 5 minutes. Stir in the prosciutto and cook, stirring, for 1 minute. Season with salt and pepper.

3 Pour the warm dressing over the spinach and basil and toss well. Sprinkle with the Parmesan and serve.

Artichoke Mousse

SERVES 4 TO 6

10 **artichokes,** trimmed, leaving only the heart
1 **lemon,** halved
Pinch of salt and pepper
1 **potato,** peeled and quartered
1½ cups heavy cream, hot
½ cup crème fraîche
3 tablespoons salt
1 tablespoon white pepper
3 tablespoons unsalted butter

1 In a large pot, simmer the artichokes with the lemon, salt, and pepper until tender.

2 In a separate saucepan, simmer the potato in salted water until tender.

3 Remove the lemon from the artichokes and drain. Transfer to a food processor.

4 Drain the potato and transfer to the food processor.

5 Process the artichokes and potatoes to a puree, slowly adding the hot heavy cream and crème fraîche.

6 Season with salt and pepper.

7 Fold in the butter.

$\mathscr{B}$aked Kumquats and Parsnips

SERVES 4

1 pound **parsnips,** peeled and cut diagonally into ¼-inch-thick slices
2 **pears,** peeled, halved, cored, and sliced
12 **kumquats,** sliced crosswise and seeds removed
4 tablespoons unsalted butter, melted
3 tablespoons fresh orange juice
3 tablespoons brown sugar

1 Preheat the oven to 350 degrees F.

2 Combine the parsnips, pears, and kumquats in a 10-inch square baking dish.

3 In a small bowl, combine the butter, orange juice, and brown sugar, and stir until smooth. Pour the mixture evenly over the parsnips and fruit. Cover with aluminum foil and bake for 45 minutes.

4 Remove the foil and bake for 15 minutes longer, or until the top is golden brown. Serve.

Balsamic-Glazed Onions with Green Beans

ℬalsamic-Glazed Onions with Green Beans

SERVES 4

1 pound **pearl onions**
1/4 cup balsamic vinegar
1 tablespoon unsalted butter
1 tablespoon vegetable oil
1 teaspoon finely chopped fresh **thyme**
1/2 teaspoon salt
1 teaspoon freshly ground pepper
1 1/2 pounds **green beans**
2 tablespoons olive oil
1 1/2 teaspoons Dijon mustard

1 Preheat the oven to 400 degrees F.

2 In a large saucepan of boiling water, blanch the onions for 1 minute. Drain and rinse under cold water. Trim the root ends, slip off the skins, and place in a large bowl.

3 In a small saucepan, combine 2 tablespoons of the balsamic vinegar, the butter, vegetable oil, thyme, 1/4 teaspoon of the salt, and 1/2 teaspoon of the pepper and stir over low heat until the butter is melted.

4 Pour the vinegar mixture over the onions and toss to coat. Spread the onions on a baking sheet and roast, stirring frequently, for about 40 minutes, or until evenly browned. Remove from the oven and reduce the oven temperature to 350 degrees F.

5 Meanwhile, in a large pot of boiling salted water, blanch the green beans until just tender, about 4 minutes. Drain, refresh under cold water, and drain again. Set aside.

6 In a large bowl, combine the olive oil, mustard, and whisk the remaining 2 tablespoons balsamic vinegar, 1/4 teaspoon salt, and 1/2 teaspoon pepper.

7 Add the the roasted onions and the green beans to the dressing and toss well. Transfer the vegetables to a large casserole. Cover and bake for about 20 minutes, or until heated through.

---

*B*arbecued Onion Salad

SERVES 4

4 large **red onions,** sliced into 1/2-inch-thick rings
1 cup plus 2 tablespoons barbecue sauce
1 tablespoon balsamic vinegar
1 tablespoon red wine vinegar
1 tablespoon rice wine vinegar
3 tablespoons olive oil
1 teaspoon Asian sesame oil
1 1/2 teaspoons minced garlic
1 tablespoon chopped fresh **thyme**
1 1/2 teaspoons salt
1 tablespoon cracked black pepper

1 Prepare a hot fire in a charcoal or gas grill.

2 Brush the onion slices on both sides with 1 cup of the barbecue sauce. Grill on both sides until just tender. Transfer to a bowl, cover, and let stand for 10 to 15 minutes.

2 Add the vinegars, the oils, the remaining 2 tablespoons barbecue sauce, the garlic, thyme, salt, and pepper. Toss well. Serve at room temperature, with grilled beef, duck, or chicken.

Braised Red Cabbage with Apples

SERVES 4

1 medium **red cabbage,** cored, quartered, and shredded
4 firm cooking **apples,** peeled, cored, quartered, and sliced
1/4 cup red wine vinegar
Salt
2 tablespoons unsalted butter
1 1/2 tablespoons olive oil
1 small **onion,** finely chopped
1 cup red wine
Freshly ground pepper to taste

1 Combine the cabbage and apples in a large bowl. Add the vinegar and a pinch of salt and toss well.

2 Heat the butter and oil in a large saucepan. Add the onion and sauté until tender but not browned, about 5 minutes. Add the cabbage and apples, stir well, and add the wine. Bring to a simmer, cover, and simmer gently until the cabbage is tender, about 40 minutes; add a little water if necessary. Season with salt if needed and pepper. Serve hot.

Carrot Couscous with Thyme

SERVES 4

3 tablespoons olive oil
2 **carrots,** coarsely grated
1 teaspoon fresh **lemon** juice
1/4 teaspoon sugar
2 cups water
2 teaspoons finely chopped fresh **thyme**
Salt and freshly ground pepper to taste
1 1/2 cups couscous

1 In a medium saucepan, heat the oil over medium heat. Add the carrots and sauté for 1 minute. Add the lemon juice, sugar, 2 tablespoons of the water, the thyme, and salt and pepper, cover, and simmer for 1 minute.

2 Add the remaining water and bring to a boil. Stir in the couscous, cover the pan, remove from the heat, and let stand for 5 minutes.

3 Fluff the couscous with a fork. Serve warm.

Corn Pudding

SERVES 4

3 ears **corn**
5 slices bacon, coarsely chopped
1 cup chopped **leek** (white and light green parts)
⅓ cup diced **red bell pepper**
2 cups heavy cream
3 large egg yolks
½ teaspoon dry mustard
¼ teaspoon Worcestershire sauce
Dash of Tabasco sauce
Salt and freshly ground pepper to taste

1 Preheat the oven to 350 degrees F.

2 Bring a large pot of water to a boil. Drop the corn into the water and cook for 5 minutes. Drain and rinse the corn under cold water. Cut the kernels from the cobs and put in a large bowl. Set aside.

3 In a small sauté pan, sauté the bacon over medium heat until crisp. Using a slotted spoon, transfer to paper towels to drain. Add the leeks and red pepper to the pan and sauté over medium heat for 5 minutes. Add to the corn.

4 Add the bacon and mix well. Spread the mixture over the bottom of a 1-quart baking dish.

5 In a medium bowl, whisk together the cream, egg yolks, mustard, Worcestershire sauce, Tabasco, and salt and pepper. Pour over the corn mixture. Bake for 45 minutes, or until set and golden brown on top. Serve hot.

Cranberry Bean Succotash

SERVES 4

2 tablespoons unsalted butter
½ cup chopped **onion**
4 ounces Canadian bacon, cut into fine julienne
2 pounds fresh **cranberry beans**
2 cups **corn** kernels (about 3 ears)
2½ cups chicken stock
1 ripe **tomato,** diced
1 teaspoon salt
Freshly ground pepper to taste
2 cups shredded **escarole**
½ cup chopped fresh **garlic chives** or regular **chives**

1 Melt the butter in a medium sauté pan over medium heat. Add the onion and bacon and sauté until the bacon is crisp, about 5 minutes.

2 Add the beans, corn, stock, tomato, salt, and pepper and bring to a simmer. Cover, reduce the heat to medium-low, and simmer for 25 minutes.

3 Stir in the escarole and cook until tender, about 5 minutes. Remove from the heat and stir in the chives. Cover and let stand for 10 minutes.

4 Adjust seasoning and serve.

Curried Spaghetti Squash

SERVES 4

1 **spaghetti squash**
2 tablespoons unsalted butter
1 **yellow squash,** cubed
1 tablespoon curry powder
2 tablespoons chopped fresh **chives**
Salt and freshly ground pepper to taste
2 tablespoons freshly grated Parmesan cheese

1 Cut the spaghetti squash in half and scrape out the seeds. Place the squash skin side up in a large pot and add water to cover by 2 inches. Bring to a boil, lower the heat, cover, and simmer until tender, about 20 minutes. Drain well.

2 Meanwhile, melt the butter in a medium skillet over medium heat. Add the yellow squash and curry powder and sauté until tender, 10 to 15 minutes. Strain off the sauce, keeping the squash. Add the chives and season with salt and pepper. Remove from the heat and cover to keep warm.

3 Using a fork, scoop out the spaghetti squash pulp and arrange the pulp on a serving platter. Top with the curried yellow squash, sprinkle with the Parmesan, and serve.

$\mathscr{D}$ill Mashed Potatoes

SERVES 4

Kosher salt for lining the baking sheet
4 large **baking potatoes,** scrubbed and pricked several times with a fork
2 tablespoons extra-virgin olive oil
1 tablespoon chopped fresh **dill**
Salt and freshly ground pepper to taste

1 Preheat the oven to 400 degrees F. Line a small rimmed baking sheet with a layer of salt about ⅛ inch thick.

2 Place the potatoes on the baking sheet and bake for about 1 hour, or until tender.

3 Split the potatoes lengthwise. Scoop out the pulp and place in a bowl. Add the remaining ingredients and mash with a fork. Serve immediately.

Note: Baking the potatoes on top of the salt layer adds a nice savory flavor.

Dilled Radishes

SERVES 4

2 tablespoons unsalted butter
2 bunches **radishes,** trimmed, washed, and patted dry
1½ teaspoons sugar
1 teaspoon red wine vinegar
1½ tablespoons chopped fresh **dill**
Freshly ground pepper to taste

1 Melt the butter in a medium sauté pan over medium heat. Add the radishes and stir to coat with the butter. Cover and cook for 4 minutes, stirring occasionally. Add the sugar and vinegar and cook, stirring, for 1 minute. Sprinkle with the dill and season with pepper. Serve immediately.

Fennel Gratin

SERVES 4

2 pounds **fennel** (2 to 3 bulbs), trimmed, quartered, and thinly sliced
   lengthwise
1 teaspoon salt
1 teaspoon freshly ground pepper
1½ cups heavy cream
¼ cup dried bread crumbs
¼ cup freshly grated parmesan cheese
1½ tablespoons unsalted butter

1 Preheat the oven to 425 degrees F. Butter an 8- by 10-inch baking or oval gratin dish.

2 Arrange the fennel slices in the prepared dish and season with the salt and pepper. Pour the cream over the fennel and sprinkle with the bread crumbs and cheese. Dot with the butter.

3 Cover the gratin with foil and bake for 20 minutes. Remove the foil and bake for about 20 minutes longer, until the cream has reduced and thickened and the top is browned. Serve warm.

Gilles's Mushrooms

SERVES 4

2/3 cup olive oil
1/2 cup water
Juice of 2 **lemons**
2 bay leaves
5 peppercorns, cracked
1 teaspoon salt
1 tablespoon tomato paste
2 pounds **mushrooms,** such as **shiitake, chanterelle, portobello,** and/or **lobster,** trimmed and thickly sliced

1 Combine the oil, water, lemon juice, bay leaves, peppercorns, and salt in a large stainless steel saucepan and bring to a boil. Add the tomato paste and simmer for about 10 minutes. Strain the broth and return to the pan.

2 Add the mushrooms, bring to a simmer, and cook until tender, about 5 minutes. With a slotted spoon, transfer to a serving bowl, and serve immediately.

Green Beans with Cashews

SERVES 4

1 1/2 pounds **green beans**
3 tablespoons unsalted butter
1/4 cup chopped fresh flat-leaf **parsley**
3/4 teaspoon salt
Freshly ground pepper to taste
1 cup **cashews,** chopped

1 Blanch the green beans in a large pot of boiling salted water until crisp-tender, about 4 to 5 minutes.

2 Meanwhile, melt the butter in a small saucepan. Stir in the parsley, salt, and pepper.

3 Drain the beans and place in a warm serving bowl. Sprinkle the cashews on top, pour the butter mixture over, and toss well. Serve.

161

$\mathscr{M}$aple-Glazed Butternut Squash

SERVES 4

2 **butternut squash,** halved and seeded
2 teaspoons salt
1 teaspoon white pepper
1/2 pound (2 sticks) unsalted butter, at room temperature
1/2 cup pure maple syrup
1 tablespoon minced garlic

1 Preheat the oven to 350 degrees F.

2 Place the squash cut side up on a baking sheet. Season with 1 teaspoon of the salt and 1/2 teaspoon of the pepper.

3 In a small bowl, combine the butter, maple syrup, garlic, and the remaining 1 teaspoon salt and 1/2 teaspoon pepper. Beat until smooth. Lightly brush the squash with some of the butter mixture.

4 Bake for approximately 45 to 50 minutes, or until fork-tender, frequently basting with the remaining butter mixture.

$\mathscr{P}$arslied Red Potatoes

SERVES 4

2 pounds **Red Bliss** or other waxy **potatoes**
2 tablespoons unsalted butter, at room temperature
2 1/2 tablespoons chopped fresh flat-leaf **parsley**
Salt and freshly ground pepper to taste

1 In a large pot of boiling salted water, cook the potatoes until tender, about 20 minutes. Drain, let cool slightly, and cut in half.

2 Transfer the potatoes to a serving bowl and toss with the butter, parsley, and salt and pepper. Serve.

Sautéed Swiss Chard with Tomatoes

Sautéed Turnips

SERVES 4

2 pounds large **turnips,** peeled and cut into ¾-inch cubes
2 tablespoons unsalted butter
Salt and freshly ground pepper to taste

1 In a medium saucepan of boiling lightly salted water, blanch the turnips until just tender, 12 to 15 minutes. Drain well.

2 In a large sauté pan, melt the butter over medium heat. Add the turnips, season with salt and pepper, and cook, tossing, until golden all over, about 15 minutes. Serve.

Sesame Snow Peas

SERVES 4

3 tablespoons Asian sesame oil
1 pound **snow peas,** trimmed
10 **scallions,** white and light green parts, chopped
1 tablespoon sesame seeds, toasted
Salt and freshly ground pepper to taste

1 Heat the sesame oil in a large sauté pan over medium heat. Add the snow peas and scallions and sauté for 3 minutes, until tender. Add the sesame seeds and salt and pepper. Cook for 2 to 3 minutes. Serve immediately.

Slow-Roasted Shallots

SERVES 4

12 **shallots,** peeled
4 cloves **garlic,** peeled
1 cup olive oil
4 sprigs **thyme**
2 sprigs **rosemary**
1 tablespoon kosher salt
1 teaspoon freshly ground pepper

1 Preheat the oven to 250 degrees F.

2 Combine all of the ingredients in a shallow baking dish and toss to mix well. Roast, stirring occasionally, for about 1½ hours, or until the shallots are soft and caramelized and are a deep golden brown.

3 Discard the herb sprigs, and serve hot with game birds, steak, chicken, or turkey.

Squash Sauté

SERVES 4

3 tablespoons olive oil
1 medium **yellow onion,** cut into thin wedges
1 medium **yellow squash,** cut into matchsticks
1 medium **zucchini,** cut into matchsticks

1 large **red bell pepper,** cored, seeded, and cut into thin strips
1 tablespoon chopped fresh oregano
Salt and freshly ground pepper to taste
¼ cup pitted Niçoise olives
½ cup crumbled **Montrachet** or other soft **goat cheese**
1 tablespoon fresh lemon juice

1 Heat the oil in a large sauté pan over medium-high heat. Add the onion and sauté until translucent, about 5 minutes. Add the yellow squash, zucchini, and red pepper and sauté until the vegetables are crisp-tender, 5 to 7 minutes.

2 Sprinkle with the oregano and salt and pepper. Stir in the olives and cheese, sprinkle with the lemon juice, and serve.

$\mathscr{S}$teamed Broccoli with Orange Sauce

SERVES 4

1 pound (2 sticks) unsalted butter
1¾ pounds (2 small bunches) **broccoli,** tough stalks trimmed
Salt
3 large egg yolks
⅓ cup fresh **orange** juice
1½ tablespoons fresh **lemon** juice
Grated zest of 1 orange

1 Cut 2 tablespoons of the butter into small cubes and refrigerate. Melt the remaining butter and keep warm.

2 Place the broccoli in a steamer basket over boiling water and sprinkle with salt to taste. Cover and steam until tender and bright green, 8 to 10 minutes.

3 Meanwhile, in a large heatproof bowl, whisk the egg yolks until thick and light-colored. Whisk in 1½ table-spoons of the orange juice, the lemon juice, and a pinch of salt. Add half the chilled butter; place over a saucepan of gently simmering water. Whisk constantly until the mixture starts to thicken. Remove from heat; whisk in rest of chilled butter until blended. Whisking constantly, add the melted butter in a thin steady stream and whisk until the sauce has increased in volume and thickened. Gradually whisk in remaining orange juice and orange zest.

4 Serve the broccoli with the hot butter sauce.

$\mathscr{S}$weet Potatoes
with Toasted Almonds

SERVES 6

⅔ cup slivered blanched **almonds**
4 pounds **sweet potatoes,** peeled and cut into 1-inch cubes
5 tablespoons unsalted butter, melted
1½ teaspoons salt
1 teaspoon freshly ground pepper
3 cups **apple cider**

1 Preheat the oven to 350 degrees F.

2 Spread the almonds on a baking sheet and toast in the oven, stirring occasionally, for 5 minutes, or until golden

Sweet Potatoes with Toasted Almonds

Capellini with Bell Peppers and Snow Peas

$\mathscr{C}$hile-Rubbed Beef Fillets

SERVES 4

¼ cup **cascabel chile** powder
2 tablespoons **ancho chile** powder
Cracked black pepper
1 tablespoon minced **garlic**
¼ cup plus 2 tablespoons olive oil
Four 8-ounce beef fillet steaks
1 tablespoon salt

1 In a shallow bowl, combine the chile powders, pepper, and garlic. Stir in the oil. Add the beef and rub the marinade all over it. Cover and marinate in the refrigerator for 2 hours.

2 Prepare a hot fire in a charcoal or gas grill or turn on the broiler.

3 Remove the beef from the marinade and season with the salt.

4 Grill or broil, turning once, for about 4 minutes for medium-rare. Serve.

$\mathscr{K}$iwi Chicken Sauté

SERVES 4

4 boneless, skinless chicken breast halves
1 teaspoon fresh **thyme** leaves, crushed
Salt and freshly ground pepper to taste
2 tablespoons unsalted butter
1/4 cup dry white wine
4 **kiwis,** peeled and thinly sliced

1 Pound the chicken between sheets of waxed paper to about 1/4 inch thick. Sprinkle with the thyme and salt and pepper.

2 Melt the butter in a large skillet over medium-high heat. Add the chicken and cook, turning once, until golden brown and the juices run clear when pierced with a knife, about 5 minutes. Remove to a warm platter and cover to keep warm.

3 Add the wine to the skillet and cook, stirring, for 1 minute, scraping up the brown bits on the bottom of the pan. Add the kiwi slices and cook, stirring gently, for about 30 seconds, until heated through. Pour the kiwi sauce over the chicken breasts and serve.

$\mathscr{L}$eek Frittata

SERVES 4

4 tablespoons unsalted butter
2 tablespoons olive oil
12 medium **leeks,** white and light green parts only, split, washed thoroughly, and cut into 1/4-inch-thick slices
2 tablespoons fresh **lemon** juice
1 teaspoon sugar
7 large **eggs**
1/2 cup crumbled **goat cheese**
Salt and freshly ground pepper to taste
4 ounces cream cheese

1 In a large sauté pan, heat 3 tablespoons of the butter and the oil over medium heat. Add the leeks and sauté until wilted. Stir in the lemon juice and sugar and cook over low heat until the leeks are tender, about 30 minutes. Remove from the heat.

176

2 Preheat the oven to 375 degrees F.

3 In a large bowl, beat the eggs with the goat cheese until smooth. Season with salt and pepper. Stir in the leeks.

4 Grease a large cast-iron skillet with the remaining 1 tablespoon butter. Pour in the egg mixture and dot with the cream cheese.

5 Bake for 45 minutes, until cooked through. Turn the broiler to high and place the tart under the broiler until lightly brown on top. Serve warm.

$\mathcal{L}$inguine with Zucchini Blossoms, Cream, and Saffron

SERVES 4

16 **zucchini blossoms**
12 ounces whole wheat linguine
3 tablespoons unsalted butter
4 large shallots, finely chopped
1 cup heavy cream
Generous pinch of saffron threads
Salt and freshly ground pepper to taste

1 Bring a large pot of salted water to a boil for the pasta.

2 Meanwhile, prepare the zucchini blossoms: Cut off their stalks, then insert your index or middle finger into each flower, and carefully break off the yellow, fleshy pistil; discard. Rinse the flowers gently in cold water, drain well, and pat dry on a cloth or paper towels. Slice crosswise into rings.

3 Add the pasta to boiling water and cook until al dente.

4 While the pasta is cooking, melt the butter in a large skillet over low heat. Add the shallots and cook, stirring, until softened, about 2 minutes. Add the zucchini blossoms and cook, stirring gently, for 30 seconds. Add the cream and saffron and simmer for 2 minutes. Add the salt and pepper.

5 Drain the pasta, add to the sauce, and stir gently. Serve.

*S*age-Rubbed Pork Tenderloin

3 tablespoons minced fresh **sage**
2 tablespoons minced garlic
2 tablespoons cracked black pepper
2 teaspoons Dijon mustard
1½ cups plus 2 tablespoons olive oil
4 pork tenderloins
1 tablespoon kosher salt

1 In a large shallow bowl, combine the sage, garlic, pepper, and mustard. Whisk in 1½ cups of the oil.

2 Add the pork tenderloins to the bowl and turn to coat. Cover and marinate in the refrigerator for 4 hours, turning occasionally.

3 Preheat the oven to 425 degrees F.

4 Remove the tenderloins from the marinade and season with the salt.

5 In a medium sauté pan, heat the remaining 2 tablespoons oil over high heat until smoking hot. Add the tenderloins and sear until well-browned on all sides, about 5 minutes. Transfer to a baking pan and roast for about 5 minutes, or until cooked to medium to medium well-done. Let rest for 5 minutes before slicing.

Smoked Salmon Pasta Puttanesca

SERVES 4 TO 6

2 tablespoons olive oil

1 medium **red onion,** sliced ¼ inch thick

8 large cloves **garlic,** chopped

1 tablespoon chopped fresh **oregano** or 1 heaping teaspoon dried oregano

Pinch of sea salt

1 teaspoon white pepper

¼ cup red wine

3 to 3½ cups canned tomatoes

2 teaspoons capers

½ cup freshly grated **Parmesan cheese,** plus additional for serving

8 ounces moist **smoked salmon,** preferably hot-smoked Northwest-style, flaked

1 Bring a large pot of salted water to a boil for the pasta.

2 Heat the olive oil in a large heavy skillet over medium-high heat. Add the red onion, garlic, oregano, salt, and white pepper. Cook, stirring, until the garlic is fragrant, 2 to 3 minutes. Stir in the red wine and bring to a boil. Add the tomatoes and bring to a boil. Reduce the heat to medium and simmer, stirring occasionally, until the sauce has thickened slightly, 5 to 10 minutes. Stir in the capers. Remove from the heat and cover to keep warm.

3 Meanwhile, add the pasta to the boiling water and cook until al dente. Drain well, and transfer to a large serving bowl. Add the cheese and toss well. Add the salmon and sauce and toss again. Serve with additional grated Parmesan and crusty French bread.

Sauces, Condiments, and Dressings

Basil Aïoli

1¼ CUPS

2 cups loosely packed fresh **basil** leaves
1 cup olive oil
2 large cloves **garlic,** chopped
1 teaspoon kosher salt, or more to taste
2 large egg yolks, at room temperature
1½ teaspoons fresh **lemon** juice
1 tablespoon water
Freshly ground pepper to taste

1 Combine the basil leaves, ¼ cup of the oil, the garlic, salt, egg yolks, lemon juice, and water in a blender and blend until smooth. With the motor running, add the remaining ¾ cup oil in a thin, steady stream. Season to taste with salt and pepper. Serve with grilled fish or cold poached shellfish.

Cilantro and Pineapple Salsa

SERVES 4

1½ cups chopped fresh **pineapple**
¼ cup chopped **red onion**
2 tablespoons chopped fresh **cilantro**
1 tablespoon fresh **lime** juice
1 tablespoon sugar
1 teaspoon minced peeled fresh **ginger**
Salt and freshly ground pepper to taste

1 In a small bowl, combine all the ingredients and mix well. Cover and chill until ready to serve. Adjust the seasoning before serving. Serve with grilled fish or poultry.

Fire-Roasted Yellow Pepper Vinaigrette

SERVES 4 TO 6

6 **yellow bell peppers,** cored, halved, and seeded
1½ cups plus 2 tablespoons olive oil
Salt and freshly ground pepper
2 tablespoons red wine vinegar
1 tablespoon Dijon mustard
2 teaspoons **garlic,** minced
2 teaspoons honey

1 Prepare a hot fire in a charcoal or gas grill.

2 Toss the peppers with 2 tablespoons of the oil and sprinkle lightly with salt and pepper. Grill, skin side down, until charred. Let cool to room temperature.

3 Put the peppers in a food processor and add the vinegar, mustard, garlic, honey, 1 tablespoon salt, and 1 teaspoon pepper. Process to a puree. With the motor running, slowly add the remaining 1½ cups oil in a thin, steady stream. Serve with any type of fish.

Gingered Fresh and Dried Fruit Compote

SERVES 4

¹/₂ cup sugar

¹/₂ cup water

3 tablespoons fresh **lemon** juice

1 tablespoon finely julienned peeled fresh **ginger**

6 **apricots,** halved and pitted

¹/₂ cup sun-dried **blueberries,** soaked in hot water until plump and drained

¹/₂ cup golden **raisins,** soaked in hot water until plump and drained

1 cup **raspberries**

3 tablespoons sliced **almonds,** lightly toasted

Mint sprigs for garnish

1 In a large heavy saucepan, combine the sugar, water, lemon juice, and ginger and bring to a simmer, stirring until the sugar dissolves. Simmer for 5 minutes.

2 Add the apricots, and spoon the syrup over them. Cover and cook over low heat until just tender, about 3 minutes.

3 Stir in the blueberries and raisins, cover, and cook for 1 minute. Remove from the heat and gently fold in the raspberries.

4 Spoon the fruit and syrup into 4 bowls. Serve warm or at room temperature, sprinkled with the almonds and garnished with mint.

*K*iwi Marmalade

1 CUP

4 **kiwis,** peeled and cut into ¹/₂-inch cubes
³/₄ cup sugar
Grated zest of 1 **lime**
2 tablespoons fresh **lime** juice

1 Combine the kiwis, sugar, lime zest, and lime juice in a deep stainless steel saucepan. Cook over medium-low heat, stirring occasionally, until thickened, about 20 minutes. Allow to cool to room temperature. Refrigerate until ready to serve.

*M*ango Chutney

SERVES 4

2 cups fresh **orange** juice
1 cup red wine vinegar
3 tablespoons minced peeled fresh **ginger**
1 tablespoon minced **jalapeños**
¹/₂ cup packed dark brown sugar
6 **mangoes,** peeled, pitted, and diced
1 tablespoon salt
1¹/₂ teaspoons white pepper
¹/₂ cup slivered fresh **mint** leaves

1 In a large stainless steel saucepan, combine the orange juice, vinegar, ginger, jalapeños, and brown sugar. Bring to a simmer over medium heat and cook until the liquid is reduced and thickened.

2 Add half of the mangoes and cook, stirring occasionally, until softened. Season with the salt and pepper and remove from the heat. Let cool, then cover and refrigerate until chilled.

3 Just before serving, add the remaining mangoes and the mint. Serve as an accompaniment to spicy food.

lum Sauce

SERVES 4 TO 6

1 tablespoon olive oil
3 **shallots,** sliced
2 cloves **garlic,** peeled
1 tablespoon minced peeled fresh **ginger**
1 pint **raspberries**
6 black **plums,** pitted and roughly chopped
4 cups plum wine
4 cups port
6 cups chicken stock
3 sprigs thyme
2 tablespoons honey
1 tablespoon kosher salt
2 teaspoons crushed red pepper flakes

1 Heat the oil in a large stainless steel saucepan over medium-high heat. Add the shallots, garlic, and ginger and sauté until lightly golden, about 1 to 2 minutes. Add the raspberries and plums and cook until they release their juices. Add the wine and port and bring to a boil. Cook until reduced by half.

2 Add the stock and thyme and bring to a boil. Cook until reduced to the consistency of a sauce, about 40 minutes. Remove from the heat.

3 Using a hand mixer, beat the sauce until smooth. Stir in the honey, salt, and red pepper flakes. Strain through a medium sieve.

4 Serve hot, with Chinese-style roast duck.

Roasted Habanero Salsa

SERVES 4

¼ cup extra-virgin olive oil
1 teaspoon minced garlic
6 ripe **plum tomatoes,** halved
Salt and freshly ground pepper to taste
10 **habanero chiles**
¼ cup fresh lime juice
¼ cup chopped fresh **cilantro**

1 Preheat the oven to 500 degrees F.

2 Combine 1 tablespoon of the oil and the garlic in a small bowl.

3 Place the tomatoes cut side up on a baking sheet and rub the garlic oil over the cut sides. Sprinkle with salt and pepper and roast for about 15 minutes, or until lightly browned. Cool to room temperature. Chop the roasted tomatoes and transfer to a bowl.

4 Meanwhile, prepare a charcoal or gas grill. Grill or broil the habaneros, turning occasionally, until lightly colored, about 3 minutes.

5 Dice the habaneros and add to tomatoes, along with the remaining 3 tablespoons oil, the lime juice, and cilantro. Mix well and refrigerate until ready to serve.

Spinach with Sizzling Lime Butter

ABOUT 2 CUPS

10 ounces **spinach,** washed and stemmed
1 pound unsalted butter, at room temperature
Grated zest and juice of 6 **limes**
1 tablespoon honey
1 cup chopped fresh **cilantro**
2 tablespoons kosher salt
1 tablespoon white pepper

1 In a large pot of boiling water, blanch the spinach just until bright green, about 1 to 2 minutes. Immediately plunge into a bowl of ice water to stop the cooking. Drain well, transfer to a blender, and puree.

2 In a medium bowl, whisk together the butter, lemon and lime juice and zest, and honey until smooth. Whisk in the spinach, then the cilantro. Whisk in the salt and white pepper.

3 Transfer to an airtight container and keep in the freezer until ready to use. Perfect for cooking chicken or fish, or spreading on hot chicken or fish just before serving.

Sun-dried–Cherry Wine Sauce

SERVES 4

2 teaspoons olive oil

3 tablespoons minced **shallots**

1 cup Pinot noir or other full-bodied red wine

¾ cup chicken stock

⅓ cup **sun-dried cherries**, soaked in hot water until plump and drained

2 tablespoons coarsely chopped fresh flat-leaf **parsley**

6 tablespoons unsalted butter

Salt and freshly ground pepper to taste

1 In a medium sauté pan, heat the oil. Add the shallots and sauté until softened, about 2 minutes.

2 Add the wine, stock, cherries, and parsley and bring to a boil. Boil until the liquid is reduced by one-half. Gradually whisk in the butter. Let boil to thicken. Serve with grilled chicken, beef, venison, or pork.

Tomatillo Vinaigrette

SERVES 4 TO 6

2 cups diced **tomatillos**

3 tablespoons minced **red onion**

1 tablespoon minced **garlic**

1 teaspoon dried oregano, preferably Mexican

2 tablespoons red wine vinegar

1 bunch **cilantro,** leaves only

2 cups olive oil

2 tablespoons honey

1 tablespoon kosher salt

2 teaspoons white pepper

1 In a blender, combine the tomatillos, red onion, garlic, oregano, and vinegar, and blend until smooth. Add the cilantro and blend well. With the motor running, slowly add the oil in a thin, steady stream. Add the honey, salt, and white pepper. Serve with salmon, swordfish, or other firm-fleshed fish.

Desserts and Baked Goods

Apricot-Raisin Bread

1 LOAF

¾ cup coarsely chopped **dried apricots**
½ cup **dark raisins**
1 cup boiling water
½ cup plus 3 tablespoons sugar
2¼ cups unbleached all-purpose flour
1 tablespoon baking powder
½ teaspoon salt
⅓ cup vegetable oil
2 large **eggs,** beaten
⅔ cup milk
¾ cup unprocessed bran flakes (available at health food stores)

1 Preheat the oven to 350 degrees F. Grease a 9- by 5-inch loaf pan.

2 Combine the apricots and raisins in a small bowl, add the boiling water, and let sit for 10 minutes. Drain well.

3 Add 3 tablespoons of the sugar to the apricots and raisins and toss well.

4 Sift the flour, baking powder, and salt together.

5 In a large bowl, combine the oil and the remaining ½ cup sugar and beat well. Add the eggs one at a time, beating well after each addition.

6 Add the dry ingredients alternately with the milk, then add the bran. Fold in the fruits.

7 Pour the batter into the prepared pan. Bake for 1 hour, or until a cake tester inserted in the center comes out clean. Let cool in the pan on a wire rack for 10 minutes, then remove from the pan and let cool completely on the rack.

$\mathscr{B}$aked Rhubarb with Raspberries

SERVES 4

1 1/3 cups **raspberries**
3/4 cup packed light brown sugar
1/4 cup hot water
1 pound **rhubarb,** trimmed and chopped
2 tablespoons unsalted butter, cut into small pieces
1/4 teaspoon vanilla extract

1 Preheat the oven to 350 degrees F.

2 Combine the raspberries, brown sugar, and water in a blender and puree. Strain the puree into a bowl.

3 Add the rhubarb, butter, and vanilla to the puree and stir to combine.

4 Scrape the mixture into a 9- by 13-inch baking dish. Bake for 15 minutes. Stir gently and bake for 15 minutes longer, or until the rhubarb is soft.

5 Let cool for 10 minutes before serving. Serve with vanilla ice cream or whipped cream.

Berry Mélange

erry Mélange

SERVES 6

1 pint **raspberries,** rinsed and patted dry
1 pint **blueberries,** rinsed and patted dry
1 pint **strawberries,** rinsed, hulled, patted dry, and halved
  or quartered if large
1 cup cassis liqueur
1 tablespoon sugar

1 In a large bowl, combine the berries. Add the cassis
and toss. Sprinkle with the sugar and toss again. Cover
and chill for at least 1 hour. Serve with vanilla ice cream
or butter cookies.

---

lueberry Tart

ONE 9-INCH TART

1 cup unbleached all-purpose flour
$1/4$ cup plus 1 tablespoon granulated sugar
8 tablespoons (1 stick) cold unsalted butter, cut into $1/2$-inch cubes
$1/2$ teaspoon vanilla extract
3 cups **blueberries,** rinsed and patted dry
Confectioners' sugar for dusting

1. Preheat the oven to 425 degrees F. Lightly grease a 9-inch tart pan with a removable bottom.

2 Place the flour and ¼ cup of the granulated sugar in a food processor and process briefly to combine. Add the butter and pulse until the mixture resembles coarse meal. Add the vanilla and process for about 1 minute, or until the dough begins to form a ball. Transfer to a lightly floured work surface and knead briefly. Shape the dough into a ball.

3 Press the dough evenly over the bottom of the pre-pared pan.

4 In a bowl, toss the blueberries with the remaining 1 tablespoon granulated sugar. Spread the berries over the dough, mounding them in the center. Bake for about 50 minutes, until the crust is golden and the juices are bubbling. Transfer to a wire rack and let cool.

5 To serve, remove the tart ring, and sift or sprinkle confectioners' sugar over the tart.

Blueberry Tart

ourbon Sabayon

SERVES 4

2 cups heavy cream
6 large **egg** yolks
1½ oz sugar
¼ cup plus 2 tablespoons bourbon
½ oz dissolved melted gelatin

1 In a large bowl, whip the cream until it holds stiff peaks. Cover and chill.

2 In a large heatproof bowl, combine the egg yolks, sugar, and bourbon and whisk until well blended.

3 Place the bowl over a saucepan of simmering water and whisk until thickened and very foamy. Whisk in the dissolved gelatin.

4 Remove from the heat and fold in the whipped cream. Serve with pumpkin pie.

Cantaloupe Sorbet

1 QUART

3½ cups water
2¼ cups sugar
1 cup **cantaloupe** juice
1 large **egg** white

1 In a medium saucepan, combine the water and sugar and heat, stirring, until the sugar is completely dissolved. Stir in the cantaloupe juice. Let cool.

2 In a small bowl, whip the egg white until frothy. Add the egg white to the cantaloupe syrup.

3 Transfer the mixture to an ice cream freezer and freeze according to the manufacturer's instructions.

Carrot Cake

SERVES 10-12

CAKE

1¾ cups plus 2 tablespoons unbleached all-purpose flour
2 teaspoons baking powder
1 teaspoon baking soda
2 teaspoons ground cinnamon
¼ teaspoon salt
1¼ cups canola oil
2 cups sugar
4 large **eggs**
5 cups grated **carrots**
1 cup toasted chopped **pecans**
1 cup golden **raisins**

ICING

½ pound (2 sticks) unsalted butter, at room temperature
8 ounces cream cheese, at room temperature
1 pound confectioners' sugar
1 teaspoon vanilla extract

1 Preheat the oven to 350 degrees F. Grease and flour a 10-inch tube pan or 12-cup Bundt pan.

2 To make the cake, sift the flour, baking powder, baking soda, cinnamon, and salt together.

3 In a large bowl, whisk the oil and sugar together. Whisk in half of the dry ingredients. Whisk in 1 of the eggs, then whisk in the remaining dry ingredients alternately with the remaining eggs. Stir in the carrots, pecans, and raisins. Scrape the batter into the prepared pan.

4 Bake for 1 hour and 10 minutes, or until a toothpick inserted into the center of the cake comes out clean. Let cool completely in the pan on a rack.

5 To make the icing, in a large bowl, using an electric mixer, beat the butter and cream cheese until smooth. Gradually beat in the confectioners' sugar. Beat in the vanilla.

6 Invert the cake onto a serving platter. Frost with the icing and serve.

Date and Fig Bars

1 cup chopped pitted **dates**
¾ cup chopped dried **figs**
3 tablespoons granulated sugar
2 tablespoons grated **lemon** zest
2 tablespoons brandy
½ pound (2 sticks) unsalted butter, at room temperature
2 cups packed brown sugar
2 large **eggs**
2 teaspoons vanilla extract
2½ cups old-fashioned rolled oats
2¼ cups unbleached all-purpose flour
1 teaspoon baking powder
2 teaspoons ground cinnamon
1 teaspoon salt
1 cup chopped toasted and peeled **hazelnuts**

1 Preheat the oven to 350 degrees F. Grease a 9-inch square baking pan.

2 In a medium saucepan, combine the dates and figs and add water to cover by 1 inch. Bring to a simmer and cook until tender, about 20 minutes. Drain well and transfer to a food processor.

3 Add the granulated sugar, lemon zest, and brandy to the fruit and process until smooth.

4 In a large bowl, cream the butter and brown sugar. Add the eggs one at a time, beating well after each addition. Beat in the vanilla.

5 Stir in the oats, flour, baking powder, cinnamon, and salt. Stir in the hazelnuts.

6 Spread two-thirds of the oatmeal mixture over the bottom of the prepared baking pan. Spread the date puree over the top. Crumble the remaining oatmeal mixture over the date puree.

7 Bake for 25 to 30 minutes, until golden brown on top. Cool completely, then cut into 16 squares.

Grapefruit Granita

1 QUART

3½ cups water
¼ cup sugar
1 cup fresh **grapefruit** juice, strained
1 large **egg** white

1 In a medium stainless steel saucepan, combine the water and sugar and heat, stirring until the sugar is completely dissolved. Stir in the grapefruit juice. Let cool.

2 In a small bowl, whip the egg until frothy. Add the egg white to the grapefruit syrup.

3 Pour the mixture into a deep stainless steel baking pan and place in the freezer. Freeze, stirring frequently with a fork to break up any large ice crystals as they form.

Hazelnut Ice Cream

2 QUARTS

2 cups milk
2 cups heavy cream
1 cup plus 2 tablespoons sugar
1 pound **hazelnuts,** toasted and peeled
2 vanilla beans, preferable Tahitian, split
8 large **egg** yolks

1 Combine the milk, cream, 1 cup of the sugar, the hazelnuts, and vanilla beans in a large heavy pot and bring just to a simmer. Remove from the heat.

2 Combine the egg yolks and remaining 2 tablespoons sugar in a medium bowl and whisk until smooth. Gradually whisk in about one-third of the hot milk mixture. Return the egg yolk mixture to the saucepan and cook over low heat, stirring constantly, until the custard thickens and coats the back of a spoon. Do not boil.

3 Strain the custard into a bowl. Set it into a larger bowl of ice water and let cool, stirring occasionally.

4 Transfer the mixture to an ice cream freezer and freeze according to the manufacturer's instructions.

$\mathscr{L}$emon-Cheese Strudel

SERVES 6

8 tablespoons (1 stick) unsalted butter, melted
1 cup sugar
1 tablespoon ground cinnamon
4 tablespoons unsalted butter, at room temperature
8 ounces cream cheese, at room temperature
1 teaspoon **lemon** zest
1/3 cup sour cream
3 large **egg** yolks
8 sheets phyllo dough, thawed

1 Preheat the oven to 350 degrees F. Lightly brush a cookie sheet with some of the melted butter.

2 Combine 1/2 cup of the sugar and the cinnamon in a small bowl. Measure out 1 tablespoon of the cinnamon sugar for the topping and set aside.

3 To make the filling, in a large bowl, using an electric mixer, beat the room-temperature butter and the remaining 1/2 cup sugar until smooth. Beat in the cream cheese and lemon zest and beat until light and fluffy. Beat in the sour cream and egg yolks until well blended.

4 Lay a phyllo sheet on a work surface with a long side facing you. Brush the phyllo sheet with butter. Lightly dust with the sugar and cinnamon mixture.

5 Repeat the process with the remaining phyllo sheets, brushing each one with butter and sprinkling with cinnamon sugar.

6 Spread the filling across the bottom of the phyllo stack, leaving a 1-inch border along the bottom edge and the sides. Fold the sides of the phyllo over the filling. Brush the folded edges and the top edge with butter and roll up jelly-roll fashion. Press the seam to seal.

7 Place the strudel seam side down on the prepared baking sheet. Brush with the remaining melted butter and sprinkle with the reserved cinnamon sugar. Bake for about 30 minutes, or until the pastry is golden and crisp. Cool slightly, then cut into slices with a serrated knife and serve.

ℒeona's Blueberry Muffins

12 MUFFINS

2 cups plus 1 tablespoon unbleached all-purpose flour
1/2 cup sugar
2 1/2 teaspoons baking powder
1/2 teaspoon salt
1/2 cup **blueberries,** rinsed and patted dry
1 large **egg**
3/4 cup milk
4 tablespoons unsalted butter, melted and cooled

1 Preheat the oven to 350 degrees F. Lightly grease 12 muffin cups.

2 Sift together 2 cups of the flour, the sugar, baking powder, and salt into a large bowl.

3 In a small bowl, toss the blueberries with the remaining 1 tablespoon flour.

4 In another small bowl, beat the egg and milk until well blended. Gradually stir into the dry ingredients. (The batter will be stiff.) Stir in the melted butter. Fold in the blueberries.

5 Pour the batter into the prepared muffin cups, filling them two-thirds full. Bake for 30 to 35 minutes, until golden brown on top. Serve warm.

ℳaple Carrot Muffins

12 MUFFINS

1¼ cups unbleached all-purpose flour
1 tablespoon baking powder
½ teaspoon ground allspice
¼ teaspoon salt
4 tablespoons unsalted butter, at room temperature
1 large **egg**
¾ cup maple syrup
1 cup milk
1 cup grated **carrots**
1 cup quick-cooking oats

1 Preheat the oven to 400 degrees F.

2 Sift together the flour, baking powder, allspice, and salt.

3 In a large bowl, beat together the butter, egg, and syrup. Stir in the milk, carrots, and oats until well blended. Stir in the dry ingredients. Do not overmix.

4 Pour the batter into 12 muffin cups, filling them three-quarters full. Bake for 20 to 30 minutes, until golden brown. Serve warm.

𝒫each Ice Cream

1 QUART

1½ cups heavy cream
½ cup sugar
9 ripe **peaches**
3 tablespoons Amaretto

1 In a medium saucepan, combine the cream and sugar and cook over low heat, stirring, until the sugar dissolves. Transfer to a bowl and let cool.

2 In a large pot of boiling water, blanch the peaches for 2 minutes. Drain and let cool, then peel, cut in half, and remove the pits.

3 Put 6 of the peaches in a food processor and process until smooth. Add the liqueur and process to combine. Add the peach puree to the cream mixture.

4 Cut the remaining 2 peaches into ¼-inch dice. Stir into the cream mixture and freeze in an ice cream maker according to the manufacturer's instructions.

𝒫umpkin-Ginger Mousse

SERVES 4

1 tablespoon unflavored gelatin
4 large **eggs**
¼ cup plus 3 tablespoons sugar
1½ cups **pumpkin** puree, preferably fresh
¾ teaspoon ground cinnamon
½ teaspoon grated fresh ginger
¼ teaspoon grated nutmeg
1 cup heavy cream

1 Place the gelatin in a small bowl and add enough water to dissolve.

2 In a large bowl, beat the eggs and sugar until thick and light-colored. Beat in the dissolved gelatin. Beat in the pumpkin puree and spices. Cover and chill until the mixture begins to set, about one hour.

3 In a medium bowl, whip the cream until it holds soft peaks. Fold the whipped cream into the pumpkin mixture.

4 Spoon the mousse into 4 dessert bowls. Cover and chill for at least 4 hours before serving.

Rich Chocolate Soufflé

SERVES 6

Sugar for coating the soufflé dish
3 tablespoons unsalted butter
3 tablespoons unbleached all-purpose flour
1½ cups milk
1 pound good-quality bittersweet chocolate, broken into small pieces
1 teaspoon vanilla
¾ cup strong brewed coffee
½ cup sugar
5 large **eggs,** separated, at room temperature
2 large **egg** whites, at room temperature
Pinch of cream of tartar
Sweetened whipped cream for serving

1 Preheat the oven to 375 degrees F. Butter a 2-quart soufflé dish and coat with sugar.

2 In a medium heavy saucepan, heat the butter over low heat until melted and foamy. Whisk in the flour; whisk for 1 minute. Gradually stir in the milk and stir until thick and smooth.

3 Add the chocolate and cook, stirring constantly, until the chocolate has melted. Stir in the coffee and remove from the heat.

4 Stir in ¼ cup of the sugar and the vanilla. Add the egg yolks one at a time, whisking well after each addition.

5 In a large bowl, beat the egg whites with the cream of tartar until foamy. Beat in the remaining ¼ cup sugar 1 tablespoon at a time, and beat until the whites are stiff and glossy. Gently fold the egg whites into the soufflé base. Pour the mixture into the prepared dish and smooth the top.

6 Bake for 40 minutes, or until puffed and lightly browned on top. Serve immediately with whipped cream.

Sautéed Apples with Brandy

SERVES 4

5 tablespoons unsalted butter
¼ cup packed brown sugar
4 **Golden Delicious apples,** peeled, cored, and sliced lengthwise
Pinch each of salt and freshly ground pepper

1 Melt the butter in a large sauté pan over medium heat. Add the brown sugar and brandy and cook, stirring, until the sugar has dissolved. Add the apples and the salt and pepper and cook until the apples are tender. Serve warm over ice cream.

$\mathscr{V}$anilla Ice Cream with Caramelized Nectarines and Blackberry Puree

SERVES 4

PUREE

1/2 cup sugar
1/2 cup water
1 pint **blackberries**
1 tablespoon fresh **lemon** juice

NECTARINES

1 cup butter
6 **nectarines,** peeled, pitted, and quartered

1 pint good-quality vanilla ice cream

1 To make the puree, in a medium saucepan, combine the sugar and water and cook over medium heat, stirring, until the sugar is dissolved. Add the blackberries and cook, stirring frequently, until the berries are very soft, 7 to 10 minutes. Transfer to a blender, add the lemon juice, and puree. Strain through a fine sieve into a bowl and refrigerate.

2 To prepare the nectarines, heat a large sauté pan over medium heat. Add 1/2 cup of the butter, then add the nectarines and cook, stirring frequently, until tender and lightly browned. Add the remaining butter. Remove from the heat.

3 Spoon the ice cream into 4 dessert bowls. Spoon the warm nectarines over the ice cream and top with the blackberry puree.

Directory

of Farmer's Markets in the U.S. and Canada

Note: Most of the markets listed are seasonal (spring to fall) unless otherwise noted. Times, days of the week, and locations are subject to change, so it is advisable to call the market office to confirm these details. If no hours are listed for a market, this means that they begin at about 8 or 9 AM and last until sell-out of that day. Most markets offer organic produce.

ALABAMA

Downtown Farmers' Market
106 Carroway & N. First Ave.
205-324-0650
Daily, year-round

Jefferson County Truck Growers Association
414 W. Finley Ave.
205-251-8737
Daily, year-round

DECATUR
Decatur/Morgan County Farmers' Market
First Ave. SE
205-351-9782

FLORENCE
Florence/Lauderdale Farmers' Market
S. Poplar St.
205-760-5896

HUNTSVILLE
Madison County Farmers' Market
1022 Cook Ave.
205-532-1661
year-round

MOBILE
Farmers' Market of Mobile County
2243 Halls Mill Rd.
334-473-9146
Daily, year-round

MONTGOMERY
Montgomery State Farmers' Market
1655 Federal Dr.
334-242-5350
Daily, year-round

TUSCALOOSA
Tuscaloosa Farmers' Market
Greensboro Ave. & River Rd.
205-349-3886, ext. 288
Tue, Sat, Spring; Tue, Thurs, Sat, Summer; Sat, Winter

ALASKA

ANCHORAGE
Anchorage Saturday Market
3rd & E St.
907-276-7207
Sat

FAIRBANKS
Tanana Valley Farmers' Market
1800 College Rd.
907-456-FARM
Wed, Noon–5PM, Sat, 9AM–4PM, May–Sep

KENAI
Central Kenai Peninsula Farmers' Market
Kobuk, between BJ Bar & Kaladi Brothers
907-283-3633, 262-6170, 262-5463
Sat, 10AM–2PM, Jun–Sep

ARIZONA

PHOENIX
Heritage Square Farmers' Market
Seventh & Monroe St.
602-848-1234
Thurs, Oct–Jul

ARKANSAS

FAYETTEVILLE
Fayetteville Farmer's Market
The Square
501-634-7122

HOT SPRINGS
Hot Springs Farmers' Market
Central Ave. in Hill Wheatley Plaza
501-337-0611

LITTLE ROCK
Downtown Farmers' Market
S. Metro Center parking deck, ground level at Scott St.
501-375-0121
Tue, 7:30AM–3PM

Home Grown Farmers' Market
Breckenridge Village
Pleasant Valley Dr. and Cantrell St.
501-868-9620
Tue

Home Grown Farmers' Market
Lakewood Village
North Little Rock
Thurs

Farmers' Market
Second Presbyterian Church
Sat, 6:30AM–Sellout

PINE BLUFF
Arkansas Vegetable Grower's Marketing Association
4th & Walnut St.
501-479-5062
Year–round

CALIFORNIA

Auburn Certified Farmers' Market
Gold Country Fairgrounds
916-823-6183
Sat, 8AM–Noon, year-round

Bakersfield Certified Farmers' Market
East Hills Mall
Gottschalk's Ct.
805-324-1863
Tue, 3PM–6PM, Sun, 1–5PM, year-round

Montgomery Ward
30th & F St.
805-324-1863
Sat, 8AM–11AM, year-round

Bakersfield Stockdale Fashion Plaza
Stockdale Hwy. at Outhouse Steak House
805-324-1863
Thurs, 3PM–6PM, Sat, 2PM–5PM, year-round

Bellflower Certified Farmers' Market
Simm's Park
Oak & Clark St.
310-804-1424
Mon, 9AM–1PM, year-round

Berkeley Certified Farmers' Market
Center St. & Martin Luther King Way
510-548-8333
Sat, 10AM–2PM, year-round

Derby St. & Martin Luther King Way
510-548-8333
Tue, 2PM–7PM

Haste St. & Telegraph Ave.
510-548-8333
Sun, 11AM–3PM, May–Nov

Beverly Hills Certified Farmers' Market
300 block of N. Canon Dr.
310-285-1048
Sun, 9AM–1PM, year-round

Burbank Certified Farmers' Market
3rd St. & Palm Ave.
818-308-0457
Sat, 8AM–1:30PM, year-round

Calabasas Certified Farmers' Market
Old Town Calabasas
818-223-8696
Sat, 9AM–1PM, year-round

Chico Certified Farmers' Market
2nd & Wall St.
916-893-FARM
Wed, 5–9PM, Jun–Sep
Sat, 7:30AM–1PM, year-round

Compton/Hub City Certified Farmers' Market
Alameda & Compton
310-537-5415
Fri, 11AM–6PM, year-round

Todos Santos Plaza
1-800-949-FARM
Sat, 9AM–1PM, Jun–Nov; Wed, 10AM–2PM, Jun–Dec

Coronado Certified Farmers' Market
1st & B St.
619-741-3763
Tue, 2:30PM–6PM, year-round

Coronado Certified Farmers' Market
Loews Bay Resort, 4000 Coronado Bat Rd.
619-424-4450
Sun, 10AM–2PM, year-round

Costa Mesa Certified Farmers' Market
Orange County Fairgrounds
714-646-8342
Thurs, 9AM–1PM, year-round

Daly City Certified Farmers' Market
Serramonte Shopping Center & I-280
1-800-949-FARM
Thurs, 10AM–2PM, year-round

DANVILLE

Danville-Blackhawk Certified Farmer's Market (Old Town)
Blackhawk Plaza
510-945-2940
Sun, 9AM–1PM, May–Nov

Danville Certified Farmers' Market
Old Town
Railroad Ave. & Prospect
1-800-949-FARM
Sat, 9AM–1PM, May–Dec

DAVIS

Davis Certified Farmers' Market
Central Park
4th & C St.
916-756-1695
Sat, 8AM–Noon, year-round;
Wed, 4:30PM–8:30PM, May–Oct;
Wed, 2PM–6PM, Nov–Apr

ENCINO

Encino Certified Farmers' Market
17400 Victory Blvd., at White Oak
818-705-2345
Sun, 8AM–Noon, year-round

EUREKA

Eureka Certified Farmers' Market
Eureka Mall on Harris St.
707-441-9699
Thurs, 10AM–1PM, Jun–Oct

Old Eureka Certified Farmers' Market
Old Town, Eureka
707-441-9699
Tue, 10 AM–1PM, Jul–Oct

FAIRFIELD

Fairfield Certified Farmers' Market
Gateway Plaza
707-425-FARM
Sun, 9AM–1:30PM, Jun–Oct

Fairfield Certified Farmers' Market
Texas & Madison St.
707-425-FARM
Thurs, 3PM–6:30PM, May–Oct

FRESNO

Fresno Farmers' Market
100 W. Shaw, at Blackstone
209-222-0182
Sat, 6AM–Noon, Wed, 2PM–6PM, year-round

FULLERTON

Fullerton Certified Farmers' Market
450 W. Orangethorpe
714-535-5694
Wed, 9:30AM–2:30PM, year-round

Fullerton Market
Wiltshire & Pomona
714-526-5814
Thurs, 4PM–9PM, year-round

GLENDALE

Glendale Certified Farmers' Market
N. Brand St., at Broadway
818-449-0179
Thurs, 9:30AM–1:30PM, year-round

HERMOSA BEACH

Hermosa Beach Certified Farmers' Market
13th St. & Hermosa Ave.
310-379-1488
Fri, Noon–4PM, year-round

HOLLYWOOD

Hollywood Certified Farmers' Market
Ivar Ave. & Hollywood Blvd.
213-463-3171
Sun, 9AM–1PM, year-round

LONG BEACH

Long Beach Certified Farmers' Market (Downtown)
The Promenade
3rd & Broadway
310-433-3881
Fri, 10AM–4PM, year-round

North Long Beach Certified Farmers' Market
51st & Long Beach Blvd.
310-433-3881
Sat, 7:30AM–11:30AM, year-round

LOS ANGELES

Los Angeles Adams & Vermont Certified Farmers' Market
St. Agnes Catholic Church
213-777-1755
Wed, 2PM–6PM, year-round

Los Angeles Certified Farmers' Market
2936 W. 8th St., at Westmoreland
818-954-9668
Mon, 1:30PM–4:30PM, year-round

MENLO PARK

Menlo Park Certified Farmers' Market
Crane & Chestnut St.
408-257-2760
Sun, 10AM–2PM, year-round

Mission Valley Farmers' Market
Friars & Frazee Rd.
619-741-3763
Year-round

Modesto Farmer's Market
16th St.
209-632-9322

Montecito Certified Farmers' Market
1200 Coast Village Rd.
805-962-5354
Fri, 8:30AM–12:30PM, year-round

Monterey Bay Peninsula College Farmers' Market
980 Fremont
408-728-5060
Thurs, 2:30PM–6:30PM, year-round

Old Monterey Marketplace Certified Farmers' Market
Alvarado St.
408-665-8070
Tue, 4PM–6PM, year-round

Mountain View Certified Farmers' Market
100 Castro St.
1-800-806-FARM
Sun, 9AM–1PM, year-round

Downtown Certified Farmers' Market
West Pearl St. parking lot
707-252-7142
Tue, 7:30AM–Noon, May–Nov

Napa Chef's Certified Farmers' Market
First & Coombs St.
707-252-7142
Fri, 4PM–8PM, May–Nov

Norwalk Certified Farmers' Market
Alondra Blvd. & Pioneer Ave.
310-863-7375
Tue, 10AM–2PM, year-round

Oakland Certified Farmers' Market
Jack London Square
1-800-949-FARM
Sun, 10AM–2PM, year-round

Old Oakland Certified Farmers' Market (Downtown)
9th St. & Broadway
415-456-3276
Fri, 8AM–2PM, year-round

Oceanside Downtown Certified Farmers' Market
North Hill & Third St.
619-258-5420
Thurs, 9:30AM–12:30PM, year-round

Ojai Certified Farmers' Market
300 E. Matilija
805-646-4444
Sun, 10AM–2PM, year-round

Orange Certified Farmers' Market
230 E. Chapman Ave., rear parking lot
714-646-8342
Sat, 9AM–1PM, year-round

Oxnard Certified Farmers' Market
5th & B St.
805-483-7960
Thurs, 10AM–1PM, year-round

Palm Springs Village Festival Certified Farmers' Market
Palm Canyon Dr. & Amado
619-320-3781
Thurs, 6PM–9PM, year-round

Palo Alto Downtown Certified Farmers' Market
Hamilton & Gilman St.
415-325-2088
Sat, 8AM–Noon, May–Nov

Palos Verdes/Rolling Hills Estates Certified Farmers' Market
Hawthorne & Silverspur
818-377-8111
Sun, 9AM–1PM, year-round

Pasadena Certified Farmers' Market
Victory Park
818-449-0179
Sat, 8AM–1PM, year-round

Pasadena Farmers' Market
City Hall
100 N. Garfield
818-449-0179
Year-round

Pasadena Farmers' Market
Villa Park, 363 E. Villa St.,
818-449-0179
Year-round

Petaluma Certified Farmers' Market
Walnut Park
707-762-0344
Sat, 2PM–5PM, Jun–Oct

Petaluma East Certified Farmers' Market
Lucchesi Park
707-762-0344
Wed, 4PM–7PM, Jun–Sep

Placerville Certified Farmers' Market
Main St., at Cedar Ravine
916-621-4772
Sat, 8AM–Noon

Thursday Night Certified Farmers' Market
Downtown Placerville
916-626-9625
Thurs, 5PM–8PM, Jul–Oct

Pleasanton Certified Farmers' Market
Main St. & W. Angela
1-800-949-FARM
Sat, 9AM–1PM, year-round

Pomona Certified Farmers' Market
Pearl at North Garey
213-735-2586
Sat, 7:30AM–11:30AM, year-round

Red Bluff Certified Farmers' Market
WalMart parking lot
916-527-4813
Sat, 8AM–Noon, Jun–Sep

Redding Certified Farmers' Market
Mount Shasta Mall
916-347-5677
Tue, Sat, 7:30AM–Noon

Redondo Beach Certified Farmers' Market
Redondo Beach Pier
310-540-0722
Thurs, 9AM–1PM, year-round

Redwood City Certified Farmers' Market
Winslow & Middlefield
415-592-4103
Sat, 7AM–Noon

Riverside Certified Farmers' Market
Riverside-Arlington Sears
909-823-1411
Fri, 9AM–1PM, year-round

Sacramento Center Certified Farmers' Market
8th & West St.
916-363-FOOD
Sun, 8AM–Noon, year-round

Sacramento Country Club Center Certified Farmers' Market
El Camino & Watt Ave.
916-363-FOOD
Tue, 8AM–11:30AM, year-round

Elk Grove Certified Farmers' Market
Elk Park Village
916-363-FOOD
Sun, 8AM–11AM, Jun–Oct

Florin Mall Certified Farmers' Market
Florin Mall, at 65th St.
916-363-FOOD
Thurs, 8AM–11:30AM, year-round

K St. Mall Certified Farmers' Market
11th & K St.
916-363-FOOD
Thurs, 5PM–9PM, May–Oct

Plaza Park Certified Farmers' Market
Plaza Park
10th & J St.
916-363-FOOD
Wed, 10AM–2PM, May–Dec

Roosevelt Park Certified Farmers' Market
Roosevelt Park
9th & P St.
916-363-FOOD
Tue, 10AM–2PM, Jun–Oct

Sunrise Mall Certified Farmers' Market
Sunrise Mall, behind Sears
916-363-FOOD
Sat, 8AM–Noon, year-round

Town & Country Certified Farmers' Market
Town & Country Village Shopping Center
916-363-FOOD
Fri, 8AM–11:30AM, Jun–Oct

ST. HELENA

Napa Valley Certified Farmers' Market
St. Helena Railroad Depot
707-963-7343
Fri, 7:30AM–11:30AM, May–Nov

SAN DIEGO

El Cajon Certified Farmers' Market
El Cajon Blvd. & Marlborough
619-258-5420
Sun, 10AM–2PM, year-round

Hazard Center Certified Farmers' Market
Friars & Frazee Rd.
619-741-3763
Thurs, 3PM–6:30PM

SAN FRANCISCO

San Francisco Certified Farmers' Market
100 Alemany Blvd.
415-647-9423
Sat, 6AM–6PM, year-round

Ferry Plaza Certified Farmers' Market
Ferry Building
510-528-6987
Sat, 8AM–1:30PM, year-round

Heart of the City Certified Farmers' Market
7th & Market St. (UN Plaza)
415-558-9455
Wed, Sun, 7AM–5PM, year-round

SAN JOSE

Blossom Hill Certified Farmers' Market
Princeton Plaza Mall
1-800-806-FARM
Sun, 10AM–2PM, Jun–Nov

Downtown Certified Farmers' Market
S. 1st & San Fernando
800-949-FARM
Thurs, 10AM–2PM, May–Nov

Japan Town Certified Farmers' Market
7th & Jackson St.
408-298-4303
Sun, 8AM–1PM, year-round

San Jose Certified Farmers' Market
Town & Country Shopping Centre
1-800-949-FARM
Sun, 10AM–2PM, Jun–Nov; Fri, 10AM–2PM, year-round

SAN LUIS OBISPO

San Luis Obispo Certified Farmers' Market
Central Coast Plaza, Gottschalk parking lot,
805-544-9570
Sat, 8AM–10:30AM

Higuera St. Certified Farmers' Market
Higuera St., at Chorro
805-544-9570
Thurs, 6:30PM–Sellout

SAN MATEO

San Mateo Certified Farmers' Market
Fashion Island Shopping Center
800-949-FARM
Wed, 10AM–2PM, year-round; Sat, 9AM–1PM, Jun–Nov

SAN PEDRO

San Pedro Certified Farmers' Market
3rd St., between Mesa & Centre
310-433-3881
Thurs, 10AM–2PM, year-round

SAN RAFAEL

Marin County Certified Farmers' Market
Marin Civic Center Hwy. 101, San Pedro exit
415-456-FARM
Thurs, Sun, 8AM–1PM, year-round

Downtown Certified Farmers' Market
4th St.
415-457-2266
Thurs, 6PM–9PM, Apr–Oct

SANTA BARBARA

Old Town Certified Farmers' Market
500 to 600 block of State St.
805-962-5354
Tue, 4PM–7:30PM, year-round

Santa Barbara Certified Farmers' Market
Coast Village Rd.
805-962-5354
Fri, 8:30AM–Noon, year-round

Santa Barbara Certified Farmers' Market
Santa Barbara & Cota St.
805-962-5354
Sat, 8:30AM–12:30PM, year-round

Santa Cruz Certified Farmers' Market
Lincoln & Cedar St.
408-429-8433
Wed, 2:30PM–6:30PM

Santa Monica Certified Farmers' Market
Arizona Ave. & 2nd St.
310-458-8900
Wed, 9:30AM–3PM, Sat,
8:30AM–Noon, year-round

Santa Monica Certified Farmers' Market
Ocean Park, at Main St.
310-458-8900
Sun, 9AM–Noon, year-round

Santa Monica Certified Farmers' Market
Pico Blvd., at Cloverdale
310-458-8900
Sat, 8:30AM–1PM, year-round

Original Certified Farmers' Market
Veterans Memorial Building parking lot
707-523-0962
Wed, 9AM–Noon

Santa Rosa Certified Farmers' Market
Montgomery Village Sonoma Ave. & Farmers' Ln.
707-538-7023
Wed, 8:30AM–11:30AM, year-round

Thursday Night Certified Farmers' Market (Downtown)
4th St.
707-769-9145
Thurs, 5PM–8:30PM, Jun–Sep

Sonoma Certified Farmers' Market
Arnold Field parking lot & 1st St.
707-538-7023
Fri, 9AM–Noon, year-round

Sonoma Certified Farmers' Market
Sonoma Plaza & Napa St.
707-538-7023
Tue, 5:30PM–Dusk

South Lake Tahoe Certified Farmers' Market
American Legion Hall, Hwy. 50
916-621-4772
Tue, 9AM–1PM

Stockton Certified Farmer's Market (Downtown)
El Dorado & San Joaquin St.
209-943-1830
Sat, 7AM–Noon, year-round

Stockton Certified Farmers' Market
March & Pacific St.
209-943-1830
Thurs, Sun, 9AM–1PM, year-round

Sunnyvale Certified Farmers' Market
Murphy & Washington St.
415-456-3276
Sat, 9AM–1PM

L.A. Mission College Certified Farmers' Markets
13356 Eldridge Ave.
818-896-6539
Sun, 8AM–2PM

Thousand Oaks Certified Farmers' Market
Village Center Square
805-529-6266
Thurs, 4PM–7PM, year-round

Torrance Certified Farmers' Market
Wilson Park
310-379-1488
Tue, Sat, 8AM–Noon, year-round

Ukiah Certified Farmers' Market
Orchard Plaza parking lot
707-743-1726
Sat, 8:30AM–Noon, May–Oct

Ukiah Certified Farmers' Market
School & Clay St.
707-743-1726
Tue, 3PM–6PM, May–Oct

Nut Tree Certified Farmers' Market
I-80, Monte Vista exit
415-456-3276
4PM-8PM, Jun–Oct

Vacaville Certified Farmers' Market (Downtown)
Main St.
415-456-3276
Sat, 8AM–Noon, year-round

Old Town Certified Farmers' Market
Georgia St. & Sonoma Blvd.
707-552-3115
Sat, 9AM–1PM, year-round

Van Nuys Certified Farmers' Market
Sylvan St., near Courthouse
818-989-5066
Sat, 8AM–Noon, year-round

Venice Certified Farmers' Market
Venice Blvd. & Ocean Ave.
310-399-6690
Fri, 7AM–11AM, year-round

Downtown Certified Farmers' Market
Santa Clara & California St.
805-529-6266
Sat, 8:30AM–Noon, year-round

Midtown Certified Farmers' Market
Montgomery Ward
Main St. & Mills
805-529-6266
Wed, 10AM–1PM, year-round

Visalia Certified Farmers' Market
K & Tulare St.
209-747-0095
Tue, 5:30PM–8:30PM, May–Sep

Downtown Certified Farmers' Market
Church & Main St.
209-747-0095
Thurs, 5:30PM–8:30PM, May–Sep

Sears Parking Lot Certified Farmers' Market
Sears parking lot
Mooney & Caldwell St.
209-747-0095
Sat, 8AM–11:30AM, year-round

Walnut Creek Certified Farmers' Market
Broadway & Lincoln St.
510-945-2940
Sun, 8AM–1PM

Westchester Certified Farmers' Market
87th & Sepulveda
310-375-5900
Wed, 8:30AM–1PM

West Covina Certified Farmers' Market
Sunset & Plaza St.
818-338-8496
Sat, 7AM–11AM, year-round

West Hollywood Certified Farmers' Market
Plummer Park
310-967-4202
Mon, 9AM–2PM, year-round

Westwood Village Certified Farmers' Market
Weyburn, at Bullock's Department Store
310-208-1984
Thurs, 3PM–7PM

Whittier Certified Farmers' Market
12000 Bailey St.
714-526-5814
Tue, 4PM–8PM, Fri 8AM–1PM, year-round

COLORADO

Vocational School
Main & Bell
Sat, 7AM–1:30PM, Aug–Oct

Fletcher Plaza
E. Colfax & Emporia
303-361-6169
Sat, 7AM–Sellout, Apr–Oct

15324 E. Hampden Circle
303-361-6169
Wed, 9AM–Sellout, Apr–Oct

Central Park
13th & Canyon Blvd.
303-494-4997
Wed, 11AM–4PM, Sat, 8AM–2PM, May–Sep

**Douglas County Farmers'
Market**
410 Fairgrounds Rd.
303-688-3096
Sat, 7:30AM–11:30AM, Jul–Oct

COLORADO SPRINGS

Acacia Park
Bijou & Nevada St.
719-598-4215
Mon, 7AM–1:30PM, Jun–Oct

Colorado Blvd. at 24th St.
719-598-4215
Sat, 7AM–1:30PM, Jun–Oct

Memorial Park
Pike's Peak Ave. & Union Blvd.
719-598-4215
Thurs, 7AM–1:30PM, Jun–Oct

WalMart near Chapel Hills Mall
719-598-4215
Sat, 7AM–1:30PM, Jun–Oct

DENVER

17th & Market St.
303-794-7768
Sat, 7AM–1PM, Jun–Oct

University Hills Market
2700 S. Colorado Blvd.
303-794-7768
Tue, 11AM–Sellout, Jun–Oct

FORT COLLINS

Larimer County parking lot, at
Mountain St.
303-484-1776
Sat, 8AM–Noon, Jul–Sep

Montgomery Ward parking lot
2201 S. College Ave.
303-484-7263
Tue, 10AM–2PM, Wed, 3PM–6PM,
Sun, 11AM–2PM, Jul–Sep

GRAND JUNCTION

Teller Arms Shopping Center
parking lot
2800 North Ave.
303-434-3531
Wed, Sat, 7AM–Noon, May–Nov

GREELEY

10th St. & 7th Ave.
Wed, 4:30PM–7:30PM, Sat,
7:30AM–11:30AM, Jul–first frost

LITTLETON

Broadridge Plaza Shopping Center
6905 S. Broadway
303-794-7768
Wed, 11AM–Sellout, Jun–Oct

LOVELAND

5th & Lincoln
Sat, 8AM–Noon, Jul–Sep

PUEBLO

Midtown Shopping Center
6th & Midtown Circle
719-545-6738
Fri, 8AM–2PM, Jul–Oct

Mineral Palace Park
15th & Santa Fe
719-546-6000
Tue, 7AM–1PM, Jul–Oct

STEAMBOAT SPRINGS

Routt County Courthouse, front
lawn, 5th & Yampa
303-879-0825
Sat, 8AM–1PM, Jun–first frost

CONNECTICUT

BETHEL

67 Stony Hill Rd.
Sat, 9AM–1PM, Jul–Oct

BLOOMFIELD

Bloomfield Town Hall
800 Bloomfield Ave.
9AM–1PM, Jul–Oct

BRIDGEPORT

Wall St.
Fri, 9AM–2PM, Aug–Oct

BRISTOL

Stock's Playground Middle St.
Sat, 10AM–1PM, Jul–Oct

DANBURY

City Center Farmers' Market
The Danbury Green, between
Delay & Ives St.
Sat, 10AM–1PM, Jul–Oct

EAST HARTFORD

Raymond Memorial Library
840 Main St.
Fri, 9AM–1PM, Jul–Oct

HARTFORD

Downtown Farmers' Market
Main & Asylum St.
Mon, Wed, Fri, Sat, 10AM–3PM,
Apr–Oct

Hartford Regional Market
Daily, 5AM–Noon, year-round

Horace Bushnell Farmers' Market
23 Vine St.
Tue, 10AM–1PM, Jul–Sep

Park Street Farmers' Market
Park & Washington St.
Mon, 10AM–1PM, Jul–Oct

South End Farmers' Market
St. Augustine Church schoolyard
Maple & Clifford St.
Thurs, 12:30PM–2:30PM, Jul–Oct

Butler St. parking lot
W. Main & Grove St.
Sat, 8:30AM–12:30PM, Jul–Oct

South Green, at Old Church St.
Tue, Fri, 8AM–1PM, Jul–Oct

Elm Terrace Farmers' Market
Dixwell Avenue Q-House
197 Dixwell Avenue
Sat, 11AM–2PM, Jul–Oct

Pitkin Plaza at Orange St.
Wed, 9AM–2PM, Sat, 9AM–1PM, Jun–Oct

224 College St.
Thurs, 10AM–2:30PM, Jul–Oct

Union Plaza, at State St.
Tue, Fri, 9:30AM–2PM, Jul–Oct

Town Hall
10 Main St.
Sat, 9AM–Noon, May–Oct

N. Water St. parking lot, at
Maritime Center
Wed, Noon–6PM, Jul–Oct

Howard T. Brown Memorial Park
Shetucket St.
Sat, 8:30AM–Noon, Jul–Oct

Salvation Army parking lot
262 Main St.
Wed, 9:30AM–Noon, Jul–Oct

Tri-Town Farmers' Market
St. Bernard's Church
Wed, 3PM–6PM, Jul–Oct

Columbus Park
Main St. & W. Park Place
Mon, Thurs, 10AM–3PM, Jul–Oct

St. Mark's Episcopal Chapel
42 N. Eagleville Rd.
Sat, 3PM–6:30PM, Jul–Oct

Torrington Plaza, across from the
Village Green
Tue, 3PM–6PM, Sat, 10AM–1PM,
Jul–Oct

Caldor's parking lot
855 Lake Wood Rd.
Thurs, 1PM–5PM, Jul–Oct

LaSalle Rd. public parking
Tue, 9:30AM–1:30PM, Thurs,
2PM–5PM, Jun–Oct

Jackson & Union St.
Tue, 2:30PM–5:30PM, Sat,
7:30a–Noon, Jul–Oct

Windsor/Wilson Farmers' Market
Metro Home Design Center
184 Windsor Ave.
Tue, 3PM–6PM, Jul–Oct

DELAWARE

Lewes Farmers' Market
1400 Hwy. 1
302-644-1135
Daily, 10AM–9PM, May–Oct; Fri,
Sat, Sun, 10AM–6PM, Nov–Apr

110 N. DuPont Hwy.
302-328-4101
Fri, Sat, 10AM–10PM, Sun,
10AM–6PM, year-round

Wilmington Farmers' Market
8th & Orange St.
Wed, Fri, Sat, 7AM–4PM, year-round

DISTRICT OF COLUMBIA

D.C. Farmers' Market
5th St. & Neal Place, NE
202-547-3142
Year–round

D.C. Open Air Farmers' Market
RFK Stadium
Oklahoma Ave. & Benning Rd.
202-728-2800

Eastern Market
7th & S. Carolina Ave., SE
202-543-7293
Year–round

The Farmers' Market
Columbia Rd. & 18th St., NW
202-573-4527
Year-round

FLORIDA

FLORIDA CITY

300 N. Krome Ave.
305-246-6335
Year-round

FORT MEYERS

2744 Edison Ave.
813-332-6910
Year-round

FORT PIERCE

3470 S. Federal Hwy.
407-468-3917
Year-round

IMOKALEE

424 New Market Rd.
813-657-3112
Year-round

POMPANO BEACH

1255 Atlantic Blvd.
305-946-6570
Year-round

PLANT CITY

1305 W. Haines Ave.
813-752-7466
Year-round

WAUCHULA

625 S. 6th Ave.
813-773-9850
Year-round

GEORGIA

ALBANY

State Farmers' Market
701 Gaines Ave.
912-430-4245

ATHENS

State Farmers' Market
2160 W. Broad St.

AUGUSTA

State Farmers' Market
1150 5th St.
706-721-3004
Year-round

CAIRO

State Farmers' Market
1110 N. Broad St.
912-377-4504

COLUMBUS

State Farmers' Market
318 10th Ave.
706-649-7448
Year-round

CORDELE

State Farmers' Market
1901 U.S. Hwy. 41N
912-276-2335

DONALSONVILLE

State Farmers' Market
U.S. Hwy. 84

FOREST PARK

State Farmers' Market
16 Forest Pkwy.
404-366-6910
Year-round

GLENNVILLE

State Farmers' Market
U.S. Hwy. 301
912-654-2070

JESUP

State Farmers' Market
U.S. Hwy. 301
912-427-5773

MACON

State Farmers' Market
2055 Eisenhower Pkwy.
912-752-1097
Year-round

MOULTRIE

State Farmers' Market
Quitman Hwy.
912-891-7240

PELHAM
State Farmers' Market
U.S. Hwy 19N

SAVANNAH
State Farmers' Market
701 U.S. Hwy. 80W
912-966-7800
Year-round

THOMASVILLE
State Farmers' Market
502 Smith Ave.
912-225-4072
Year-round

TIFTON
State Farmers' Market
U.S. Hwy. 41
912-386-3143

VALDOSTA
State Farmers' Market
1500 S. Patterson St.

IDAHO

BOISE
Downtown Boise Farmers' Market
300 N. 6th St.
208-336-0267
Public Market
8th St. Market Place
208-344-0619

IDAHO FALLS
Growers' Market of Idaho Falls
1515 N. Gate Mile
208-529-1390

McCALL
McCall Farmers' Market
1624 E. Lake St.
208-634-3078

MOSCOW
Moscow Farmers' Market
Downtown
208-883-7036

NAMPA
Nampa Farm & Garden Market
1111 E. Locust Ln.
208-466-9337

Valley of Peace Farmers' Market
19921 Canada Rd.
208-286-9319

POCATELLO
Southeast Idaho Farmers' Market
Downtown
208-238-2778

TWIN FALLS
1227 11th Ave. East
208-734-7134

SANDPOINT
Farmers' Market at Sandpoint
431 S. 4th Ave.
208-263-8957

ILLINOIS

AURORA
44 E. Downer Place
708-844-3640

CHAMPAIGN
Old Farm Farmers' Market
303 S. Mattis
217-352-3182

115 N. Nell
217-359-0736

CHICAGO
Chicago Farmer's Market—
Austin
5600 W. Madison
312-744-4006
Back of the Yard
1200 W. 47th & 4700 S. Justine
312-744-4006
Englewood
64th & Peoria
312-744-4006
Gately
10300 S. Cottage Grove
312-744-4006
Lawnsdale
1200 S. Homan & 3400 W. Roosevelt
312-744-4006
Lincoln Park
2000 N. Halsted
312-744-4006
Lincoln Square
Lincoln & Leland St.
312-744-4006
Logan Square
63rd & Halsted
312-744-4006
Morgan Park/Beverly
Third Baptist Church of Chicago
95th & Ashland
312-744-4006

North Chicago
6200 N. Leavitt
312-744-4006

Six Corners
Clover St.
312-744-4006

South Shore
2000 E. 71st & 7100 S. Jeffrey
Blvd.
312-744-4006

South Chicago
2900 Martin Luther King Dr.
312-744-4006

COUNTRY CLUB HILL

183rd & Pulaski Ave.
708-799-8171

DE KALB

**Duck Soup Co-op Farmers'
Market**
129 E. Hillcrest
815-756-7044

EVANSTON

Maple Ave.
312-866-2936

FOREST PARK

St. Bernadine Farmers' Market
7246 W. Harrison St.
312-366-0839

HIGHLAND PARK

Ravinia Farmers' Market
477 Roger Williams Ave.
708-432-5570

HILLSDALE

Moline Farmers' Market
31701 122nd Ave. North
309-658-2593

KANKAKEE

Kankakee Farmers' Market
R.R. 6
815-935-1700

MOLINE

**Quad City Fruit & Vegetable
Growers**
5000 23rd Ave.
309-476-8284

OAK PARK

1 Village Hall Plaza
708-383-6400

PEORIA

Metro Centre
4700 N. University, at Metro Mall
309-692-6690

SKOKIE

**Village of Skokie Farmers'
Market**
5127 Oakton St.
708-673-0500

SPRINGFIELD

Springfield Farmers' Market
Downtown Square
217-789-2225

URBANA

**Lincoln Square Farmers'
Market**
Lincoln Square

INDIANA

BLOOMINGTON

Community Farmers' Market
E. 6th St. parking lot
812-331-6431
Sat, 7AM–Noon, May–Oct

EVANSVILLE

Pennsylvania & 1st Ave.
812-426-5468

FORT WAYNE

Barr St. Market
700 Barr St.
219-432-3037
Wed–Fri, 10AM–5PM, May–Oct

GREENFIELD

Greenfield Farmers' Market
Greenfield Courthouse
317-462-1113
Sat, 9AM–12:30PM, May–Jun;
Wed & Sat, 9AM–12:30PM, Jul–Oct

LAFAYETTE

5th St. between Main & Columbia
St.
317-742-2313
Tue, Thurs, Sat, 6AM–12:30PM,
May–Oct

LA GRANGE

Community Farm Market
Downtown
219-463-3914
Sat, Morning, Jul–Oct

MADISON

Courthouse Square
E. Main & Jefferson St.
812-265-8317
Tue, Thurs, Sat, 6AM–Noon,
May–Nov

NEW ALBANY

Market & Bank St.
812-941-0018
Tue, Thurs, Fri, 9AM–1PM,
Sat, 7:30AM–1PM, May–Oct

NORTH MANCHESTER

Downtown Farmer's Market
209 E. Main
219-982-2557
Tue & Sat, 8AM–Sellout, May–Oct

PLAINFIELD

**Hendricks County Farmer's
Market**
U.S. 40 & Sr 267
West end of Plainfield Plaza
317-745-5102
Sat, 8AM–Noon, Jun–Sep

RENSSELAER

Courthouse Square
219-866-5741
Sat, 7AM–Noon, Jun–Oct

RICHMOND

N. E St. & N. 8th St., by the depot
317-935-3721
Tue, 9AM–1PM, Sat, Dawn–2PM,
Jun–Oct

SOUTH BEND

1105 Northside Blvd.
219-282-1259

TELL CITY

City Hall
Main St., between 7th & 8th St.
812-547-7028
Sat, 7:30AM–Noon, Jun–Oct

Twilight Towers Senior Citizens'
Housing Project
1648 19th St.
812-547-7028
Wed, 7:30AM–10AM, Jun–Oct

VALPARAISO

Porter County Courthouse Square
219-465-0706
Tue, Thurs, 7AM–5:30PM, Jun–Oct

WARSAW

**Kosciusko County Farmers'
Market**
West end of County Fairgrounds
1400 E. Smith St.
219-267-4170
Mon, Wed, 2:30PM–5:30PM, Sat,
7AM–Noon, May–Oct

IOWA

ADAIR

City Park Shelter
515-742-3824
Fri, 4PM–5PM, Jun–Aug

AMES

North Grand Mall parking lot,
north of J. C. Penney
515-233-6648
Sat, 8AM–Noon, May–Oct; Wed,
4PM–7PM, Jun–Oct

AUDUBON

East side of City Park
712-563-4239
Thurs, 5PM–7:30PM, Jun–Oct

BOONE

**Boone Farmers' Market
Association**
WalMart parking lot
S. Story St. & Hwy. 30
515-432-4480
Thurs, 2PM–6PM, Jun–Nov

BURLINGTON

Downtown Farmers' Market
200 block of Jefferson St.
319-752-0015
Mon, 9AM–1PM, Jul–Aug

CEDAR FALLS

**Black Hawk Village Farmers'
Market**
South side of University Ave.
319-232-3773
Wed, 2PM–5PM, May–Oct

Cedar Falls Farmers' Market
South side of Overman Park, at
3rd St.
319-266-5944
Sat, 8AM–Noon, May–Oct

CEDAR RAPIDS

Cedar Rapids City Market
Riverside Roundhouse
1350 A St. SW
319-398-5175
Tue, Thurs, 3PM–6PM, Sat,
5AM–11:30AM, May–Oct

Noelridge Farmers' Market
Collins Rd. & Council St.
319-398-5175
Fri, 3:30PM–6:30PM, May–Oct

CENTERVILLE

West side of Town Square
515-437-4102
Sat, 8:30AM–9:30AM, May–Sep

CORNING

Green Hills Produce Farmers' Market
Central Park
515-322-4726
Thurs, 4PM–5:30PM, May–Sep

COUNCIL BLUFFS

River City Farmers' Market
Midlands loading dock Kanesville & Main
712-825-3611
Wed, Sat, 8AM–1PM, Jun–Sep

DAVENPORT

Downtown Davenport Association Farmers' Market
Parking lot, north of Stadium River Dr., between Gaines & Western Ave.
319-787-2429
Wed, Sat, 8AM–1PM, May–Oct

Mississippi Valley Growers Association
Parking lot on River Dr., at Western Ave.
319-587-8409
Wed, Sat, 8AM–1PM, May–Oct

DES MOINES

Downtown Farmers' Market
Court Ave. & 4th St.
515-245-3880
Sat, 7AM–1PM, May–Oct

Valley Junction Farmers' Market (West Des Moines)
West side of 100 & 200 blocks on 5th St.
515-222-3642
Thurs, 4:30PM–7PM, May–Oct

DUBUQUE

Between Central & Iowa on 13th St.; & on Iowa, between 11th & 14th St.
319-588-4400
Sat, 6AM–Noon, May–Oct

ELGIN

City Park
319-426-5387
Thurs, 5PM–7PM, Sat, 9AM–11AM, Jun–Sep

EVANSDALE

Evansdale Farmers' Market
3520 LaFayette St.
319-234-2157
Wed, 3PM–6PM, Sat, 1:30PM–3:30PM, Jun–Oct

GRINELL

Central Park, on Broad St.
515-236-6555
Thurs, 3PM–6PM, Jun–Oct

IOWA CITY

Lower level of Chauncey Swan parking ramp, between Washington & College St.
319-356-5110
Wed, 5:30PM–7:30PM, Sat, 7:30AM–11:30AM, May–Oct

IOWA FALLS

500 block of Washington Ave.
515-648-4033
Wed, 4PM–7PM, Sat, 8:30AM–11:30AM, May–Oct

KEOKUK

Keosippi Mall Parking Lot
300 Main St.
319-524-5055
Sat, 7AM–Noon, May–Oct

OTTUMWA

Municipal parking lot, next to hydro plant off 3rd St.
515-684-8303
Wed, 4PM–7PM, Sat, 7:30AM–10:30AM, May–Oct

SIOUX CITY

Siouxland Farmers' Market
923 3rd St., adjacent to Convention Center
Sun, Tue, Wed, Fri, Sat, 7AM–4PM, Jul–Sep

SPIRIT LAKE

Lakes Area Farmers' Market
Dickinson County Fairgrounds
507-662-5232
Wed, Sat, 8AM–Noon, Jun–Sep

WATERLOO

Crossroads Farmers' Market
Crossroads Shopping Center, near J. C. Penney
319-296-1840
Tue, Thurs, 3:30PM–7PM, May–Oct

Downtown Waterloo Farmers' Market
Homeland Bank parking lot, between E. 4th & Park Ave.
319-233-7049
Sat, 8AM–Noon, May–Oct

WEST BURLINGTON

Westland Mall Farmers' Market
Westland Mall parking lot
319-753-2891
Wed, Sat, 9AM–3PM, Jun–Oct

KANSAS

ABILENE

South parking lot of Courthouse
913-263-2681
Sat, 7AM–Noon, Jun–Sep

ATCHISON

North side of 400 block of Main
St., South row of parking lot
913-367-5560
Sun, Noon–10PM, year-round

FORT SCOTT

3rd & National
316-223-3065
Wed, 3:30PM–5:30PM, May–Oct

National & Old Fort Blvd.
316-223-5560
Sat, 6:30AM–9AM, May–Oct

HAYS

South parking lot of Courthouse
12th & Main
913-628-9430
Sat, 8AM–11AM, Jun–Oct

HUTCHINSON

115 S. Main
316-665-8041
Fri, 9AM–1PM, year-round

JUNCTION CITY

100 block of W. 5th, at S.
Heritage Rd.
913-762-1976
S, 7:30AM–Noon, May–Oct

LAWRENCE

City parking lot
10th & Vermont
913-842-3883
Tue, Thurs, 4PM–6:30PM, Sat,
6:30AM–10:30AM, May–Nov

LIBERAL

County Courthouse parking lot
316-624-5604
Sat, 7:30AM–Sellout, Jun–Sep

MANHATTAN

Cico Park
913-537-1602
Wed, 4PM–7PM, May–Oct

5th & Humboldt
913-537-1602
Sat, 8AM–1PM, May–Oct

MEDICINE LODGE

Hereford House Restaurant
Hwy. 160 & 281
316-886-3971
Sat, 8AM–Noon, Jun–Aug

NEWTON

Bank parking lot
527 Main
913-284-6930
Thurs, 5PM–8PM, Aug–Sep

Nortehast corner of 1st &
Grandview
316-284-6930
Sat, 7:30AM–Noon, Jun–Oct

PRATT

202 E. 1st
316-672-5503
Sat, 6AM–Sellout, Apr–Dec

RUSSELL

Courthouse parking lot
3rd & Kansas St.
913-483-2415
Sat, 8AM–11AM, Jun–Oct

SHAWNEE

City Hall parking lot
Johnson Dr. & Neiman
913-631-8917
Sat, 7AM–4PM, Sun, 8AM–4PM,
Jun–Oct

TOPEKA

1011 SW Kansas Ave.
913-232-5272
Sat, 10:30AM–11AM, May–Nov

Southeast corner of 10th &
Topeka Blvd.
913-234-9336
Sat, 7:30AM–Noon, May–Oct

WICHITA

Old Town
First St. & Mosley
316-262-3555
Wed, 8AM–2PM, Sat, 7AM–5PM, Sun,
10AM–5PM, May–Oct

Sedgewick County Extension
Education Center
21st & Ridge
316-796-1932
Sat, 7AM–Noon, May–Oct

KENTUCKY

U.S. 60, at Kentucky Farmers
Branch Bank
606-739-5184

BOWLING GREEN

State St.
502-842-1681

CARROLLTON

**Interstate Produce Farmers'
Market**
I-64
502-255-7197

COVINGTON

**Northern Kentucky Farmers'
Market**
Downtown
606-689-7961

FRANKFORT

Farm Bureau Building parking lot
Wilkinson Blvd.
502-223-7616

LEXINGTON

Vine St.
502-863-1517

LOUISVILLE

Crescent Hill Methodist Church
Frankfort Ave.
502-896-0396

PADUCAH

2nd St. & Broadway
502-443-6619

PARIS

Ardery Place
606-987-2764

SHELBYVILLE

Tri-County Farmers' Market
Midland Shopping Center
U.S. Rte. 60W
502-633-1144

WEST LOUISVILLE

1616 Rowan St.
502-778-2815

LOUISIANA

ALEXANDRIA

Alexandria Farmers' Market
500 Upper 3rd St.
318-473-1151
Tue, Thurs, Sat, 6AM–2PM, year-
round

BASTROP

**Morehouse Parish Farmers'
Market**
307 E. Madison Ave.
Mon–Sat, 7:30AM–5PM, year-round

BELLE CHASSE

Plaquemines Citrus Co-op
414-393-0776
Mon–Sat, 8AM–Sellout, Sep–Feb

COLFAX

**Grant Parish Produce
Association**
318-627-3747
Mon–Sat, 7AM–5:30PM, Jun–Jul

DE RIDDER

Beauregard Parish Fairgrounds
318-463-3825
Wed, Sat, 7AM–11AM, Jun–Sep

HOMER

Hwy. 79 S
317-927-2232
Mon, Tue, Thurs, Fri, Sat,
7AM–Noon, May–Sep

JEANERETTE

Jeanerette Airport
318-276-5069
Tue, Thurs, Sat, 7AM–Noon,
Jun–Sep

LAFAYETTE

**Acadiana Farmers' Market
Association**
801 Foreman Dr.
318-984-9057, 233-1770
Mon–Sat, 7AM–Noon, May–Sep;
Tue, Thurs, Sat, 7AM–Noon,
Oct–Apr

MONROE

Monroe Farmers' Market
Behind Civic Center
318-343-5387
Daily, 7AM–7PM, Jun–Oct

NATCHITOCHES

N.A.A.A. Farmer's Market
318-357-0819
Mon, Wed, Fri, 6AM–2PM, Jun–Aug

French Market
1100–1200 N. Peters St.
504-522-2621
Daily, open 24 hrs., year-round

Macon Ridge Growers's Association
318-428-2622
5 to 7 days per week, 8AM–Sellout, Jun–Jul

State Landry Farmers' Association
Hwy. 190 East
318-942-5761, 826-3901
Tue, Thurs, Sat, 7AM–Noon, year-round

Lincoln Parish Farmers' Market
318-368-9230
Mon, Wed, Sat, 7AM–Noon, May–Sep

Ark-La-Tex Market
Louisiana State Fairgrounds
318-635-1362
Tue, Thurs, Sat, 6AM–Sellout, Jun–Sep

Madison Parish Farmers' Cooperative
318-574-3457
Mon–Fri, 8AM–Sellout, May–Sep

Evangeline Parish Farmers' Market
230 Court St.
318-363-5646
Tue, Fri, 7AM–4PM, Jun–Aug

Franklin Parish Produce Association
Hwy. 15 & Taylor St.
318-435-5818
Mon, Tue, Wed, Fri, Sat, 8AM–5PM, May–Aug

MAINE

Auburn Mall Farmers' Market
Turner St. side of Auburn Mall
207-786-2976
Thurs, 3PM–7PM, Sat, 9AM–1PM, May–Nov

Augusta Farmers' Market
Downtown Augusta
207-737-2872
Wed, 9AM–Noon, May–Oct

Turnpike Mall
Western Ave.
207-737-2872
Sat, 9AM–1PM, May–Oct

Bath Farmers' Market
Downtown, in Fleet Bank parking lot
207-582-2213
Sat, 9AM–1PM, May–Oct

Penobscot Bay Growers' Association
Reny's parking lot
Junction of Rtes. 1 & 3
207-722-3447
Tue, Fri, Sat, 9AM–1PM, May–Oct

Bethel Farmers' Market
Rte. 26 & Railroad. St.
207-836-3217
Sat, 9AM–Noon, Jun–Oct

Blue Hill Fairgrounds
207-374-5038
Sat, 9AM–11:30AM, Jun–Sep

Conley's Garden Center
Rte. 27
207-737-8834
Thurs, 9AM–Noon, Jun–Sep

Bangor Brewer Farmers' Market
Brewer Auditorium
207-989-6732
Tue, Wed, Thurs, Fri, Sat, 7AM–Noon, May–Oct

BRUNSWICK

Brunswick Mall, on the Green
207-442-8195
Tue, Fri, 8AM–4PM, May–Nov

Cook's Corner Mall
207-442-8195
Sat, 8AM–1PM, May–Nov

CAMDEN

Colcord St., across from Tibbets
Industries
207-273-2809
Wed, 4:30PM–6:30PM, Sat, 9AM–1PM,
May–Oct

CORNISH

Pike Hall
Downtown, on Rte. 25
207-625-7145
Sat, 9AM–1PM, May–Oct

DAMARISCOTTA

Foster's Antiques
Rte. 1
207-763-3849
Fri, 9AM–1PM, May–Oct; Mon,
9AM–Noon, Jul–Aug

DEXTER

Episcopal Church parking lot
Fri, 9AM–6PM, Jun–Oct

ELLSWORTH

High St., next to Irving's Mainway
207-667-3420
Mon, Thurs, 2PM–5:30PM, Sat,
9:30AM–12:30AM, Jun–Oct

FARMINGTON

Sandy River Farmers' Market
Rte. 2
207-778-3903
Fri, 9AM–1PM, May–Oct

FORT KENT

St. John Valley Farmers' Market
Market & Main St.
207-543-6205
Sat, 7AM–1PM, May–Sep

GARDINER

Water St.
207-582-2213
Daily, 3PM–6PM, Jun–Oct

HOULTON

Rte. 1, south of I-95 next to
McDonald's
207-794-8306
Daily, Morning–Sellout, May–Oct

MACHIAS

Machias Valley Farmers' Market
At the dike on Rte. 1
207-255-4773
Sat, 8AM–Noon, May–Oct

MT. VERNON

Mt. Vernon Village
207-293-2954
Sat, 9AM–Noon, Jun–Sep

NEWPORT

Bear's One-Stop parking lot
Rte. 7N
207-368-4381
Fri, Sat, Sun, 7AM–7PM, Jun–Oct

ORONO

UMO Campus, Steam Plant parking lot
207-866-4784
Tue, Sat, 7AM–Sellout, May–Oct

PERRY

**Sunrise County Farmers'
Market**
Perry Municipal Building
Rte. 1
207-454-7091
Sat, 9AM–5PM, Jun–Sep

PHIPPSBURG

Town Hall parking lot
Rte. 209
207-389-1565
Sat, 9AM–1PM, Jun–Labor Day

PORTLAND

Portland Public Market
Monument Square, at Congress St.
207-874-8608
Mon, Wed, 7AM–2PM, Apr–Nov

Deering Oaks Park
207-874-8608
Sat, 7AM–Noon, Apr–Nov

PORTSMOUTH, NH
(administered by Maine
Federation of Farmers' Markets)

Parrot Ave. parking lot
207-439-2837
Sat, 9AM–1PM, May–Nov

RANGELEY

Upper Main St.
207-265-2600

ROBBINSTON

**Sunrise County Farmers'
Market**
Rte. 1, at Bridge Rd.
207-454-7091
Wed, 9AM–5PM, Jun–Sep

ROCKLAND

Harbor Plaza
207-785-3521
Thurs, 9AM–Noon, Jun–Sep

SACO

**Saco Farmers' Market &
Artisans' Market**
Spring St., at Saco Valley
Shopping Center
207-929-5318
Wed, Sat, 7AM–Noon, May–Oct

SANFORD

Midtown Mall
207-324-0331
Fri, 8AM–1PM, May–Oct

SPRINGVALE

Springvale Commons
207-324-0331
Wed, Sat, 8AM–1PM, May–Oct

WATERVILLE

Front St., by Two Penny Bridge
207-426-8066
Fri, Sat, 9AM–5PM, Apr–Oct

WESTBROOK

Parking lot on Wayside Dr.,
behind Rite-Aid
207-854-0624
Thurs, Fri, 6AM–6PM, Apr–Nov

YORK

Jefferds Tavern parking lot Rte. 1-A
207-363-4974
Sat, 9AM–Noon, May–Sep

MARYLAND

ANNAPOLIS

Arundel Center
Calvert St.
410-222-7434

ANNE ARUNDEL

**Anne Arundel County Farmers'
Market**
Riva St. & Harry S Truman Pkwy.
410-222-7434
Tue, Thurs, Sat, 7AM–Sellout,
Apr–Dec

BALTIMORE

Downtown Farmers' Market
Holiday & Saratoga St., under the
JFK viaduct
410-753-8632
Sun, 8AM–Noon, Jun–Dec

Gardenville Farmers' Market
St. Anthony's Church parking lot
410-488-0653
Sat, 7:30AM–Noon, Jun–Nov

Highlandtown Farmers' Market
3700 Fleet St.
410-325-9535
Year-round

Howard Park Farmers' Market
Woodbine & Liberty Heights Ave.
410-522-6222
Sat, 6AM–1PM, Jun–Dec

Irvington Farmers' Market
4021 Frederick Ave.
410-644-1904

**Park Heights Community
Farmers' Market**
Park Heights, at Pimlico Race
Course
410-466-6162
Wed, Noon–6:30PM, Jun–Nov

32nd Street Farmers' Market
Charles Village / Waverly
400 block of E. 32nd St.
410-243-1287
Sat, 7AM–Noon, Jun–Nov

BETHESDA

**Montgomery Farm Women's
Co-op Market**
7155 Wisconsin Ave.
301-652-2291
Wed, Sat, 7AM–3PM, Jun–Oct

**National Institutes of Health
(NIH) Farmers' Market**
9000 Rockville Pike, parking lot
41-B
301-217-2345
Tue, 2PM–6PM, May–Nov

CHARLOTTE HALL

Farmers' Market & Auction
Rte. 5
301-884-3108
Year-round

COLLEGE PARK

Calvert Rd. Farmers' Market
5211 Calvert Rd.
301-567-4375
Sat, 7AM–Noon, May–Nov

CUMBERLAND

**Allegheny Mountain Fresh
Farmers' Market**
Pedestrian Mall
301-724-3320

FREDERICK

Everedy Square and Shab Row Farmers' Market
Church & East St.
301-662-4140

Frederick Fairgrounds
E. Patrick St.
301-663-5895

GAITHERSBURG

8 Summit Ave.
301-218-2345
Thurs, 3PM–7PM, Jun–Nov

Upcounty Community Center Farmers' Market
8201 Emory Grove Rd.
301-217-2345

HAGERSTOWN

City Farmers' Market
W. Church St.
301-790-3200, ext. 154
Sat, 5AM–11AM, year-round

Hagerstown City Market
11 W. Church St.
301-790-3200
Year-round

Washington County Farmers' Market
Halfway & Massey Blvd., parking lot behind Massey Auto Group
301-432-8076
Wed, 4–7PM, Jun–Oct; Sat, 10AM–1PM, Jul–Oct

HYATTSVILLE

Prince George's Plaza Farmers' Market
3500 East-West Hwy.
301-559-8844

OCEAN CITY

Shore Fresh Farmers' Market
142nd St. & Coastal Hwy.
800-492-5590

Shore Fresh Farmers' Market
Phillips Restaurant parking lot
42nd & Coastal Hwy.
410-524-4647
Thurs, 8AM–1PM, May–Oct

OWINGS MILLS

New Town Farmers' Market
9320 Lakeside blvd.
410-823-4700
Tue, 11AM–3PM, Jul–Oct

PIKESVILLE

110 Sudbrook Ln.
410-653-5019
Wed, 11AM–3PM, Jul–Oct

POTOMAC

Presbyterian Church Market
10301 River Rd.
301-217-2345
Thurs, 1PM–4:30PM, May–Nov

PRINCE FREDERICK

Calvert County Farmers' Market
Adam's The Place for Ribs
3 miles south of Prince Frederick, on Rte. 231 & Rte. 4 S.
800-331-9771
Wed, 3PM–7PM, Sat, 9AM–4PM, Sun, 1PM–6PM, Apr–Oct

ROCKVILLE

Growers Only Farmers' Market
Rockville Town Center
301-309-3335
Wed, 11AM–2PM, Sat, 9AM–1PM, Jun–Oct

SALISBURY

Shore Fresh Farmers' Market
Civic & Glen Ave.
410-742-1334
Sat, 8AM–1PM, Apr–Nov

Downtown Shore Fresh Farmers' Market
Calvert St.
800-492-5590

SILVER SPRINGS

Fairland Farmers' Market
7th Day Adventist parking lot
Rte. 29 & Randolph Rd.
301-680-6530
Fri, 1PM–3PM, Jun–Nov

Fenton St. & Pershing Ave.
301-217-2345
Wayne Ave. & Fenton St., behind armory
301-217-2345
Sat, 7AM–1PM, Apr–Nov

TAKOMA PARK

Old Town
Laurn Ave., between Eastern & Carroll St.
301-270-1700
Sun, 10AM–2PM, Apr–Nov

TOWSON

Allegheny Ave. between Washington & York Rd.
410-825-1144
Thurs, 11AM–3PM, Jun–Oct

**Carroll County Farmers'
Market**
Smith Ave., at Westminster
Agricultural Center
410-875-2158
Sat, 8AM–2PM, Jun–Sep & Nov–Dec

**Downtown Westminster
Farmers' Market**
Sherwood Square parking lot
410-239-7503
Sat, 8AM–12:30PM, Jul–Sep

MASSACHUSETTS

AMHERST

Spring St. parking lot
413-253-3729
Sat, 7:30AM–1:30PM, May–Nov

ATTLEBORO

**Downtown Attleboro Farmers'
Market**
Gilbert Perry Square
508-226-0504
Sat, 8AM–Noon, Jun–Oct

BARRE

Barre Common
508-355-2853
Sat, 9:30AM–12:30PM, May–Oct

BERKSHIRE

**Berkshire Area Farmers'
Market**
Allendale Shopping Center
413-499-1012

BOSTON

Copley Square Farmers' Market
Copley Square, along St. James St.
617-727-3018, ext. 175
Tue, Fri, 11AM–6PM, Jul–Nov

**Franklin Park Community
Farmers' Market**
Franklin Park Rd., next to main
entrance of zoo
617-4442-2002
Sun, 2PM–5PM, Jul–Oct

Scollay Square Farmers' Market
Boston City Hall Plaza
(Government Center)
617-727-3018
Mon, Wed, Noon–6PM, Jul–Nov

South End Farmers' Market
Columbus Ave. & Holyoke St.
617-262-5310

BRIGHTON

Bank of Boston parking lot
5 Chestnut Hill Ave.
617-254-6100
Sat, 11:30AM–6PM, Jul–Oct

BROCKTON

Brockton Fairgrounds
508-678-8180
Sat, 10AM–3PM, Jul–Oct

City Hall Plaza
508-824-3554
Fri, 8:45AM–3PM, Jul–Oct

BROOKLINE

Coolidge Corner, Harvard St.
municipal parking lot
617-739-1228
Thurs, 1:30PM–Dusk, Jun–Oct

BUZZARDS BAY

Main St., Bourne
508-636-6228
Mon, Fri, 10AM–3PM, Jun–Sep

CAMBRIDGE

**Central Square Farmers'
Market**
Parking lot at Norfolk & Bishop
Allen St.
617-648-5117
Mon, Noon–6PM, May–Nov

**Charles Square Farmers'
Market**
Harvard Square, in front of
Charles Hotel
617-864-1200
10AM–2:30PM, Jun–Nov

CHARLESTOWN

Thompson Square Main & Austin
St.
617-241-8866
Wed, 3PM–7PM, Jul–Oct

CHARLTON

Mass Pike Farmers' Market
5E Service area
617-727-3018, ext. 175
Thurs, Fri, Sat, Sun, Mon (holi-
days), 10AM–5PM, Jun–Oct

Mass Pike Farmers' Market
6W Information Service Area
617-727-3018, ext. 175
Thurs, Fri, Sat, Sun, Mon (holi-
days), 10AM–5PM, Jul–Nov

CHELSEA

Chelsea Square, in front of Police
Station
617-889-8266
Sat, 10AM–2PM, Jun–Oct

DENNISPORT

Village Green
508-394-3747
Wed, 3PM–7PM, Jun–Oct

DORCHESTER

Fields Corner Farmers' Market
Purity Supreme parking lot, Park
St.
617-825-9126
Sat, 9AM–Noon, Jul–Oct

EAST BOSTON

London St., mini-park on Tunnel
Authority land
617-567-3227
Tue, 10AM–3PM, Jul–Oct

EASTHAMPTON

Union Plaza
413-527-5989
Tue, 2:30PM–6:30PM, May–Oct

FALL RIVER

Kennedy Park
508-880-1372
Sat, 7:30AM–1:30PM, May–Nov

Ruggles Park
508-880-1372
Wed, 9AM–3:30PM, Jun–Oct

FALMOUTH

Peg Noonan Park, near the Library
Main St.
508-548-8778
Thurs, Fri, Sat, 8AM–3PM, May–Oct

FRAMINGHAM

St. Tarcisius Church parking lot
508-435-4147
Wed, 3PM–6PM, Sat, 9AM–Noon,
Jun–Oct
Rte. 9 Farmers' Market
Caldor's & Ken's Steak House
parking lot
Rte. 9
413-731-8820
Thurs, Noon–5PM, May–Oct

GREAT BARRINGTON

Former railroad station on Castle
St.
413-229-2283
Sat, 8:30AM–12:30PM, May–Oct

GREENFIELD

Court Square
413-774-7480, 773-8342
Sat, 8AM–12:30PM, May–Oct

HAVERHILL

Main St. & Bailey Blvd.
508-372-9798
Sat, 8:30AM–1PM, Jul–Oct

HINGHAM

Hingham Harbor
Station St. lot
617-749-4643
Wed, Sat, 10AM–2PM, May–Oct

HOLYOKE

Chestnut St., between Dwight &
Hampden St.
413-534-3376
Thurs, 2:30PM–6PM, May–Nov

JAMAICA PLAIN

Bank of Boston parking lot Centre
St.
617-522-1892
Tue, Noon–6PM, Jul–Oct

LAWRENCE

Appleton Way
508-794-2320
Wed, 8AM–3PM, Jun–Oct

LEE

Town parking lot, off Main St., by
the Post Office
413-229-2283
Fri, 4PM–7:30PM, May–Oct
**Mass Pike Eastbound Farmers'
Market**
617-727-3018
Thurs, Fri, Sat, Sun & Mon (holi-
days), 10AM–5PM, Jul–Oct

LYNN

Downtown Farmers' Market
MBTA Garage
Market & Broad St.
617-598-4000
Thurs, 11AM–3PM, Jul–Oct

LOWELL

JFK Center City Hall Plaza
508-459-0551
Fri, 8:30AM–3:30PM, Jun–Oct

MANCHESTER-BY-THE-SEA

Rear of railroad station parking lot
508-388-4470
Mon, 1PM–5PM, Jun–Oct

MARLBORO

Parking lot at Bolton St. & Rte. 20
508-365-5926
Thurs, 2–6PM, Jun–Oct

Brooklawn Park
508-636-6228
Sat, 9AM–1PM, Jun–Oct

NEWTON HIGHLANDS

Cold Spring Park
Beacon St.
617-552-7120
Tue, 2PM–6PM, Jul–Oct

NORTHAMPTON

Gothic St.
413-527-3603
Sat, 7AM–12:30PM, May–Nov

NORTH ADAMS

Berkshire Plaza Artery & Holden
St.
413-663-3735
Sat, 8:30AM–Sellout, Jul–Sep

ORLEANS

Cape Cod Five Operations Center
19 W. Rd.
508-225-0951
Sat, 8AM–2PM, May–Oct

PALMER

Walnut St. parking lot
413-283-2614
Sat, 8AM–Noon, May–Oct

PITTSFIELD

Allendale Shopping Center Rte. 8
413-499-1012
Wed, Sat, 8AM–2PM, May–Oct

Downtown Farmers' Market
Columbus Ave. parking lot
413-443-6501
Fri, 10AM–2PM, Jun–Sep

QUINCY

John Hancock parking lot
Quincy Center, across from
Courthouse
617-479-1601
Fri, 11:30AM–5PM, Jun–Oct

ROXBURY

**ABCD Parker Hill/Fenway
Farmers' Market**
Brigham Circle
Osco Drug parking lot
617-445-6000
Thurs, Noon–3PM, Jul–Oct

Dudley Square Farmers' Market
On the Plaza, between Library &
Police Station
617-427-3599
Tue, Noon–6PM, Jul–Oct

SAUGUS

**Cliftondale Square Farmers'
Market**
Cliftondale Square
617-233-1855
Tue, 10AM–3PM, Jul–Oct

SOMERVILLE

Davis Square, Day & Herbert St.
parking lot
617-648-5117
Wed, Noon–6PM, Jun–Oct

SPRINGFIELD

Downtown Farmers' Market
Civic Center
413-732-5767
Wed, Fri, 10AM–2PM, May–Oct

**East Longmeadow Grange
Farmers' Market**
20 Baldwin St.
413-783-0287
Sat, 9AM–2PM, May–Oct

**Springfield Cooperative
Farmers' Market**
Avocado St.
413-786-9817
Sat, 8AM–Noon, Apr–Nov

TAUNTON

Downtown municipal parking lot
508-880-4960
Thurs, 3PM–7PM, Jul–Oct

WALTHAM

Fleet Bank parking lot
Main & Moody St.
617-893-0361
Sat, 10AM–3PM, Jun–Oct

WEST SPRINGFIELD

Westfield Farmers' Market
Center of Town Common
413-739-1458
Sat, 8AM–Noon, May–Oct

WEST TISBURY

Agricultural Hall
State Rd.
508-693-5669
Wed, 3–6PM, Sat, 9AM–Noon,
Jun–Oct

WILLIAMSTOWN

Spring St. parking lot
413-458-4988
Sat, 8AM–11:30AM, May–Oct

WORCESTER
Green Island Farmers' Market
Green Island section near Kelly
Square
508-779-6423
Sat, Sun, 9AM–1PM, Jul–Oct

Worcester Common
413-731-8820
Mon, Fri, 9:30AM–2PM, Jun–Oct

MICHIGAN

ANN ARBOR

3 Blocks away from Central
Business District
313-761-1078
Wed, 7AM–3PM, May–Dec; Sat,
7AM–3PM, year-round

BATTLE CREEK

22931 North Ave.
616-963-8394
Wed, Sat, 8AM–1PM, Jun–Oct

BAY CITY
Bay County Market
108 Adams St.
517-893-0541
Tue, Thurs, 2PM–8PM, Jul–Nov

CHEBOYGAN

County Building
616-627-8815
Sat, 8AM–1PM, Jul–Sep

DETROIT
Detroit Eastern Market
2934 Russell St.
313-833-1560
Tue, 5AM–Noon, Sat, 5AM–6PM,
year-round

FLINT
City Market
313-766-7449
Tue, Thurs, Sat, 7AM–6PM, year-
round; Fri (Fish Market) 10PM–6PM,
year-round

GRAND RAPIDS

Fulton St.
616-456-3211
Tue, Wed, Fri, Sat, 7AM–5PM,
Apr–Dec

Monroe Mall
616-774-7124
Thurs, 9AM–2:30PM, May–Nov

KALAMAZOO
Bank Street Market
616-385-8002
Tue, Thurs, Sat, 6AM–6PM,
May–Dec

Kalamazoo Mall
616-385-8002
Mon, Wed, Fri, 10AM–6PM,
May–Oct

LANSING
City Market
333 N. Cedar
517-483-4300
Daily, 7AM–5:30PM, May–Oct;
8AM–5:30PM, Nov–Apr

LIVONIA

Wilson Barn
3300 Civic Center Dr.
313-477-6229
Sat, 8AM–1PM, Jul–Oct

MUSKEGON

700 Yuba
616-726-3251
Tue, Thurs, Sat, 7AM–4PM, Jun–Nov

MUSKEGON HEIGHTS

City Hall
616-733-0124
Wed, Fri, Sat, 7AM–4PM, May–Dec

PONTIAC
**Oakland County Farmers'
Market**
Downtown
313-858-5495
Sat, 6:30AM–1PM, Jan–Apr; Tue,
Thurs, Sat, 6:30AM–1PM, May–Oct;
Thurs, Sat, 6:30AM–1PM, Nov–Dec

PORT HURON
Blue Water Farmers' Market
313-329-9358
Thurs, 8AM–Sellout, Aug–Nov

Downtown
313-385-8843
Sat, 9AM–4PM, Jul–Nov

ROYAL OAK

Downtown
313-548-8822
Sat, 7AM–1PM, Jan–Apr; Tue, Fri,
Sat, 7AM–1PM, May, Oct; Tue,
Thurs, Fri, Sat, 7AM–1PM, Jun–Sep;
Fri, S, 7AM–1PM, Nov–Dec

SAGINAW

Baum & Federal Ave.
517-759-1670
Tue, Fri, 8AM–2PM, Jul–Oct

Old Town Farmers' Market
S. Michigan & Court St.
517-793-3960
Sat, 7:30AM–2PM, Jul–Oct

Saginaw Fairgrounds
517-753-4408
Tue, Thurs, Sat, 7AM–Noon,
Jun–Nov

Downtown
906-632-7021
Sat, 8AM–3PM, Jul–Oct

Downtown
616-223-7591
Wed, Sat, 8AM–1PM, May–Oct

Depot Square, old railroad freight
house
313-483-1480
Sat, Wed, 7AM–3PM, Jun–Oct; Sat,
8AM–2PM, Nov–May

MINNESOTA

Prairie Visions Farmers' Market
507-582-7878
Fri, 9AM–Sellout, Jun–Oct

K-Mart parking lot
2310 Hwy. 29S
612-763-6893
Tue, Thurs, Sat, 9AM–Noon,
Jun–Aug; Tue, Thurs, 9AM–5PM,
Sep–Oct

Anoka County Farmers' Market
2nd Ave. & Jackson St.
612-257-4746
Thurs, 2PM–6PM, May–Oct

North Country Farmers' Market
Pine Ridge Mobil Station
950 Paul Bunyan Dr. NW
218-751-0883
Wed, Sat, 9AM–4PM, Jun–Oct

Anoka County Farmers' Market
St. Timothy's Catholic Church
707 89th Ave. NE
612-257-4746
Sat, 7AM–Noon, May–Oct; Tue,
2PM–6PM, Jul–Sep

Lakes Area Growers' Market
Westgate Mall parking lot
Hwy. 210W
218-829-8181
Tue, Fri, 8:30AM–3PM, Jun–Oct

Community Athletic Complex
8700 Zane Ave. North
612-493-8335
Tue, Fri, Noon–5:30PM, May–Oct

Mary, Mother of the Church
3333 Cliff Rd.
612-227-6856
Thurs, Noon–5PM, May–Oct

Anoka County Farmers' Market
Immaculate Conception Church
4030 NE Jackson St.
612-257-4746
Thurs, 2PM–6PM, May–Oct

Anoka County Farmers' Market
Epiphany Catholic Church
11001 NW Hanson Blvd.
612-457-4746
Wed, 2PM–6PM, Jul–Oct

1330 E. 3rd St.
218-724-9955
Wed, Sat, 7AM–Noon, May–Dec

Faribault Area Farmers' Market
Central Park
507-334-8474
Sat, Morning, Jun–Oct

Sibley County Farmers' Market
Fifth St. & Main Ave.
612-237-2866
Wed, 3PM–6PM, Jun–Oct

WalMart
Hwy. 169S
Wed, Sat, 8AM–Noon, Jun–Oct

Har Mar Mall
County Rd. B & Snelling Ave.
612-227-6856
Tue, 8AM–12:30PM, Jun–Oct

HIGHLAND PARK
St. Leo's Farmers' Market
2055 Bohland
612-227-6856
Thurs, 8AM–11AM, Jun–Oct

HOPKINS
16 9th Ave. South
612-934-1316
Sat, 7:30AM–Noon, Jun–Oct

LAKEVILLE
Lakeville Area Farmers' Market
Holyoke Ave.,
612-463-3577
Sat, 8:30AM–Noon, May–Oct

LEROY
Prairie Visions Farmers' Market
507-324-5729
Sat, 9AM–Sellout, Jun–Oct

LITTLE FALLS
Bay St.
612-632-5155
Wed, Sat, Early morning–
Afternoon, Jun–Oct

MANKATO
Madison East Shopping Center
1400 Madison Ave.
507-345-4494
Tue, Thurs, 4PM–6PM, Sat,
8AM–Noon, May–Oct

MAPLE GROVE
**Grove Square Merchants'
Association**
I-94 & Weaver Lake Rd.
612-323-1289
Thurs, 2PM–7PM, May–Oct

MINNEAPOLIS
Minneapolis Farmers' Market
I-94, exit 230
612-333-1718
Daily, 6AM–1PM, Apr–Dec

Nicollet Mall
612-333-1718
Thurs, 6AM–6PM, May–Nov

West Lake St. & Lyndale Ave.
South
612-822-8533

MONTEVIDEO
Across from Pioneer Village
612-269-6789
Thurs, 1PM–8PM, Sat, 7AM–1PM,
Jun–first frost

MOORHEAD, MN & FARGO, ND
Community Farmers' Market
Dike East Park
218-498-0216
Tue, Thurs, Sat, 10AM–6:30PM,
Jun–Oct

NORTHFIELD
**Northfield Area Farmers'
Market**
Riverside Park at 7th St.
Tue, Fri, 11:45AM–Sellout, Sat,
9AM–Sellout, May–Oct

PINE ISLAND
Main St.
507-356-8103
Sat, 8AM–Noon, Jun–Oct

RICHFIELD
Veteran's Memorial Park
64th & Portland Ave.
612-861-9385
Sat, 7AM–12:30PM, May–Oct

ROCHESTER
Downtown Farmers' Market
City Hall parking lot
507-280-0591
Sat, 8AM–Noon, May–Oct

ST. JAMES
**Watonwan County Farmers'
Market**
Downtown Park
507-375-3333
Thurs, 2PM–5:30PM, Jun–Oct

ST. PAUL
Aldrich Arena Farmers' Market
1850 White Bear Ave.
612-227-6856
Wed, 8:30AM–12:30PM, May–Nov
St. Luke's Farmers' Market
Lexington Ave., between Summit
& Portland
612-227-6856
Fri, 1:15PM–5PM, May–Nov
**St. Paul Wednesday Farmers'
Market**
290 E. 5th St.
612-227-6856
Wed, 2PM–5PM, Jul–Sep
**St. Paul Weekend Farmers'
Market**
290 E. 5th St.
612-227-6856
Sat, 6AM–1PM, Apr–Nov; Sun,
8AM–1PM, May–Oct

Seventh Place Mall Market
Seventh Place, between Wabasha
& St. Peter
612-227-6856
Thurs, 10AM–2PM, Jun–Oct; Tue,
10AM–2PM, Jul–Sep

Signal Hills Farmers' Market
Signal Hills Shopping Center
S. Robert St.
612-227-6856
Fri, 8AM–Noon, Jun–Oct

Marketfest
Washington Square
612-429-8535
Thurs, 6AM–9PM, Jun–Aug; Fri,
9AM–3PM, Jul–Oct

Under Interstate Bridge, between
2nd & 3rd St.
715-946-3932
Sat, 7:30AM–2PM, Jun–Oct; Wed,
8AM–1PM, Jul–Sep

MISSISSIPPI

Farmers' Curb Market
107 Beverly Lane
601-583-9954

Hattiesburg Produce Market
906 Hardy St.
601-544-1742

Farmer's Central Market
352 Woodrow Wilson
601-354-6573
Mon–Sat, 8AM–6PM, Sun, 1–6, year-
round

Meridian Area Farmers' Market
1800 Main St.
601-482-9764

Meridian Farmers' Market
908 25th St.
601-482-9845

South Side Curb Market
2605 C St.
601-483-0923

Adams County Farmers' Market
201 Liberty Rd.
601-445-8201

**Lafayette County Farmers'
Market**
Bramlet Building
601-234-9803

**Neshoba County Farmers'
Market**
301 1/2 W. Church St.
601-683-6461

1435 E. Main St.
601-842-9722

MISSOURI

**Jackson County Farmers'
Market**
Truman Rd.
816-252-4968

Cole County Farmers' Market
Capital Mall parking lot
314-584-3385

Jefferson City Farmers' Market
Washington Park
314-634-6482

5th & Main St. (off I-70)
816-421-0053
Year-round

The Market Place
Bridge & Ridge St.
816-288-3223
Year-round

Junction 60 & Pine Blvd.
314-686-8616

Soulard Farmers' Market
7th & Lafayette
314-622-4180
Year-round

**University City Market in the
Loop**
6655 E. Delmar St.
314-727-9625
Year-round

Ozark Farmers' Market
WalMart parking lot
417-264-7824

UNIONVILLE

North Central Missouri Farmers' Market
Center shelterhouse in City Park
816-947-2705

MONTANA

BILLINGS

4515 Rimrock Rd.
406-252-3441

BOZEMAN

608 7th Ave. South

GREAT FALLS

17 Irish Acres
406-453-5874

HAVRE

Hi-Line Farmers' Market
542 5th St. North
406-265-4754

HELENA

941 Wilder Ave.
406-442-1355

KALISPELL

4290 Farm to Market Rd.
406-755-5326

MISSOULA

917 Parkview Way
406-721-2351

NEBRASKA

KEARNEY

Kmart parking lot
308-236-1235
Sat, 8AM–Noon

LINCOLN

Haymarket Farmers' Market
Downtown Haymarket District
402-435-7496
Sat, 8AM–12:30PM

Foundation Garden
1417 N St.
402-435-7496
Wed, 10:30AM–1:30PM

NORTH PLATTE

The Mall Farmers' Market
North Platte Mall parking lot
308-239-4248
Tue, Sat, 8AM–1PM

North Platte Farmers' Market
6th & Bailey St.
308-532-7469
Sat, 7AM–Noon

North Platte Farmers' Market
Parade Plaza 6th & Dewey
308-532-7469
Tue, Noon–6PM

OMAHA

Early Bird Garden Market
4816 S. 60th
402-731-3901
Wed, 4–7PM, Sat, 8AM–1PM

Omaha Farmers' Market
Old Market parking lot
11th & Jackson St.
402-345-5401
Sat, 8AM–12:30PM, May–Oct

Rockbrook Shopping Center
108th & Center
402-345-5401
Thurs, 5PM–8PM, Jul–Aug

NEW HAMPSHIRE

CHICHESTER

Chichester Sunrise Farmers' Market
Beside Barrett Electric, on Rte. 28N
603-435-7260
Wed, 3:30–6PM, Sat, 9AM–Noon, Jun–Oct

COLEBROOK

Blue Seal parking lot
43 Colby St.
603-237-4430
Sat, 9AM–11AM, Jul–Oct

CONCORD

New Dartmouth Bank
N. State St.
603-753-4849
Sat, 9AM–Noon, May–Nov

DOVER

Rite-Aid parking lot
Chestnut St.
603-642-3381
Wed, 2:30PM–5:30PM, Jun–Oct

DURHAM

Community Church of Durham parking lot
Main St.
603-642-3381
Mon, 2:30–5:30PM, Jun–Oct

EXETER

Swasey Pkwy.
603-642-3381
Thurs, 2:30PM–5:30PM, Jun–Oct

FARMINGTON

Main St. School
Junction of Rtes. 153 & 75
603-755-2208
Sat, 8AM–1PM, May–Oct

FRANCONIA

Dow Strip, Downtown Franconia
603-823-7176
Alternate Sat, 9AM–1PM, Jul–Sep

HANCOCK

In the horse sheds behind the church
603-525-4728
Sat, 9AM–Noon, Jun–Sep

JAFFREY

Monadnock Plaza
Rte. 202
603-532-6561
Sat, 9AM–1PM, Jul–Sep

KEENE

Gilbo Ave.
603-357-0134
Tue, Sat, 9AM–2PM, May–Oct

LACONIA

Belknap Mill parking lot
Beacon St. East
603-267-7551
Sat, 8:30AM–Noon, Jun–Oct

LOUDON

Next to Fox Pond Plaza
Rte. 106
603-798-4161
Sat, 9AM–Noon, Jun–Sep

MANCHESTER

Open Air Farmers' Market
Agway parking lot
Beech & Valley St.
603-432-2978
Sat, 6AM–Noon, Jun–Nov

MILFORD

Mt. Vernon St.
603-654-6002
Sat, 9AM–Noon, Jun–Oct

NORTH HAVERHILL

Agway, on Rte. 10
603-787-2446
Sat, 10AM–2PM, Jun–Oct

PORTSMOUTH

Parrott Ave. parking lot, at South Mill Pond
603-642-3381
Sat, 9AM–1PM, May–Nov

WARNER

Warner Area Farmers' Market
Warner Town Hall lawn
603-456-2319
Sat, 9AM–12:30PM, Jun–Oct,
Christmas Fair in Nov

NEW JERSEY

BERLIN

41 Clementon Rd.
609-767-1284

LAKEWOOD

Rte. 70 Farmers' Market
201-269-1188

MORRISTOWN

Morris & Spring St.
201-285-8303

NEWARK

Newark Farmers' Market
Joseph St.
201-589-7214
Year-round

Market Square Farmers' Market
275 W. Market St.
201-355-5458

NEW BRUNSWICK

Harvest Square Farmers' Market
New & Joyce Kilmer Ave.
201-745-3443

NORTH PLAINFIELD

Somerset & Race St.
908-756-7665

PATERSON

Paterson Market Growers
Railway Ave.
201-742-1019
Year-round

SOUTH AMBOY

New Jersey Tailgate Farmers' Market
Garden State Parkway, near exit 124
201-442-8600

SOUTH ORANGE

Main Street Farmers' Market
4 Main St.
201-763-6899

Village Farmers' Market
Sloan St.
201-763-6899

960 Spruce St.
609-695-2998
Year-round

Montclair Farmers' Market
Glenridge & Forrest Ave.

Cowtown Farmers' Market
Rte. 40
609-769-3000
Year-round

NEW MEXICO

County Fairgrounds
401 Fairgrounds Rd.
505-437-0231

Albuquerque Growers' Market
Caravan East parking lot
7605 Central Ave. NE
505-265-7250
Village Growers' Market
City Hall & Fire Station
505-897-9104

Eddy Plaza Growers' Market
San Jose Plaza
505-887-6595

**Five State Producer Growers'
Market**
Hwy. 87 & 1st St.
505-374-9361

Highland Shopping Center
21st St.
505-763-6505

Big Rock Shopping Center
Hwy. 78
505-753-5340

W. Arrington Ave.
505-327-2814

Downtown Mall
505-526-0383

Mill & Grant St.
505-454-1497

Central Ave.
505-662-6594

Main St. & Don Pasqual Pkwy.
505-865-9561

North Valley Growers' Market
Haynes Park
528 19th St.
505-867-2951

Sanbusco Market Center
505-983-4098

Grant County Farmer's Market
Hwy. 180W
505-388-5284

County Courthouse
505-758-3982

NEW YORK

**Downtown Albany Farmers'
Market**
Pine St. & Broadway
518-732-2991
Thurs, 11AM–2PM, May–Nov
**Empire State Plaza Farmers'
Market**
North end of Empire State Plaza,
between L.O.B. & Judicial
Building
518-677-3474
Wed, Fri, 11AM–2PM, Apr–Oct
**Evangelical Protestant Church
Farmers' Market**
Clinton & Alexander St.
518-439-4363
Wed, 11AM–2PM, Jun–Nov
**Holy Cross Church Farmers'
Market**
10 Rosemont St. near Western Ave.
518-732-2991
Wed, 2:30–6PM, May–Oct

Jolly Farmers' Market
4th Ave. & S. Pearl St.
518-439-4831
Wed, 9AM–2PM, Jun–Oct

First Congregational Church Farmers' Market
405 Quail St., at Maple
518-439-4363
Sat, 9AM–Noon, Jun–Oct

Pine Grove Farmers' Market
Methodist Church
1580 Central Ave.
518-732-2991
Fri, 3PM–6PM, Jun–Oct

Sacred Heart Church Farmers' Market
31 Walter St., at N. Pearl
518-439-4363
Fri, 11AM–2PM, Jun–Oct

State Campus Farmers' Market
Harriman State Campus
Behind Building 8A
518-677-3474
Thurs, 11AM–1PM, Apr–Oct

St. Vincent's Farmers' Market
900 Madison Ave.
518-439-4363
Tue, 11AM-2PM, Jun–Oct

Third Reformed Church Farmers' Market
Whitehall Rd. & Kate St.
518-439-4363
Thurs, 3PM–6PM, Jun–Oct

Whitney Young Farmers' Market
Lark & Marshall Dr.
518-439-4363
Fri, 2:30PM–5:30PM, Jul–Oct

YWCA Farmers' Market
Lincoln & Colvin Ave.
518-439-4363

Hamer-Campos Farmers' Market
JHS 198 schoolyard
Beach 56th St.
718-883-4117
Sat, 8AM–4PM, Jun–Oct

Farmers' Co-op Market of Cayuga County
Genesee St., between Loop Rd. & South St.
315-497-2874
Tue, Thurs, Sat, 7:30AM–2PM, Jun–Oct

Finger Lakes Mall
315-255-1188
Fri, 8AM–1PM, Jun–Oct

Genessee County Farmers' Market
Main St.
716-343-9491
Tue, Fri, 9AM–5PM, Jun–Oct

Washington St., between Court & Hawley St.
607-772-8860
Tue, Fri, 8AM–2:45PM, Jul–Oct

Bronx Sunday Market
Joyce Kilmer Park
Grand Concourse & 163rd St.
718-884-5716
Sun, 10AM–5PM, Jul–Oct

Healthy Start Farmers' Market
Alexander Ave. & 139th St.
800-281-2889
Thurs, 8AM–6PM, Jul–Oct

Healthy Start Farmers' Market
Forest Ave. & 156th St.
800-281-2889
Wed, 8AM–6PM, Jul–Oct

Lincoln Hospital Greenmarket
149th St. & Park Ave.
212-477-3220
Tue, Fri, 8AM–3PM, Jul–Nov

People's Park Farmers' Market
1702-1710 Southern Blvd., between 173rd & 174th St.
718-842-0256
Fri, 9AM–6PM, Jul–Oct

Poe Park Greenmarket
Grand Concourse & 192nd St.
212-477-3220
Tue, 8AM–2PM, Jun–Nov

Brookhaven National Lab Farmers' Market
Employees' parking lot
516-722-8097
Wed, 11:30AM–1:30PM, May–Nov

Albee Square Greenmarket
Fulton St. & DeKalb Ave.
212-477-3220
Wed, 8AM–4PM, Jul–Nov

Borough Hall Greenmarket
Borough Hall Plaza, at Court St.
212-477-3220
Tue, Sat, 8AM–6PM, Year-round

Graham Ave. Farmers' Market
Graham & Cook St. dead end near P.S. 257
718-387-6643

**Grand Army Plaza
Greenmarket**
Grand Army Plaza entrance to
Prospect Park
Union St. & Prospect Park West
212-477-3220
Sat, 8AM–4PM, year-round

BUFFALO

Downtown Country Market
Main St., between Court &
Division St.
716-856-3150
Thurs, 8AM–2:30PM, May–Oct

**Niagara Frontier Growers'
Market**
1443-1517 Clinton St.
716-822-2466
Daily, 5AM–5PM, year-round

999 Broadway
rear parking garage
716-893-0705
Sat, 7AM–3PM, May–Oct

CANANDAIGUA

Downtown Farmers' Market
716-396-0300
Wed, Jul–Oct

**Hanna Junction Farm & Craft
Market**
Hanna Rd.(1 mile north of town
on Rte. 21)
716-394-7740
Thurs, 10AM–8PM, Apr–Dec

CATSKILL

Hill & Bridge St.
518-622-9820
Sat, 10AM–2PM, Jun–Oct

Rte. 9W parking lot
518-622-9820
Tue, 10AM–2PM, Jun–Oct

CHAUTAUQUA

**Chautauqua Institution
Farmers' Market**
Main Gate building, Rte. 394
716-357-6264
Mon–Sat, 7AM–11AM, Jun–Aug

COOPERSTOWN

Leatherstocking Garage, off Main
St.
607-547-8881
Sat, 8AM–1PM, May–Oct

ELMIRA

Carousal Farm & Craft Market
Eldridge Park, off Woodland Ave.
607-737-5750
Tue, 10AM–7PM, May–Sep

FREDONIA

**Village of Fredonia Farmers'
Market**
Village Hall parking lot
716-679-2302
Sat, 8AM–Noon, Jun–Oct

GLENS FALLS

Cronin Highrise parking lot
518-677-3474
Thurs, 3PM–6PM, Jun–Oct

Elm St. parking lot
518-677-3474
Sat, 7AM–Noon, May–Oct

GOSHEN

Church Park Square
914-294-7741
Fri, 10AM–5PM, May–Nov

GREENWICH

Western Auto
Rte. 29
518-854-3750
Tue, Thurs, 2PM–6PM, Jun–Oct

HAMILTON

Village Green
315-824-1111
Sat, 8AM–1PM, May–Oct

HARTSDALE

**Town of Greenburgh Farmers'
Market**
Train Station, parking area
914-347-5648
Sat, 8AM–6PM, Jun–Oct

HAUPPAUGE

State Campus Farmers' Market
State Office Campus
Veterans Memorial Hwy.
516-360-6222
Thurs, 11AM–5:30PM, Jun–Oct

HUDSON

7th Street Park
7th & Columbia St.
518-828-9458
Sat, 8AM–5PM, May–Oct

HUDSON FALLS

Ames parking lot
184 Burgoyne Ave.
518-677-3473
Wed, 10AM–1PM, Jun–Sep

ISLIP

Islip Growers' Market
Town Hall parking lot
655 Main St.
516-581-4576

Sat, 8AM–2PM, Jun–Nov

Dewitt Park
607-273-8015
Tue, 9AM–1PM, Apr–Dec

Pyramid Mall
607-257-5337

345 3rd St., at steamboat landing
607-273-8015
Sat, 9AM–2PM, Sun, 10AM–2PM,
Apr–Dec

Forest Ave. & Weir Ln.
516-581-4576
Sat, 8AM–1PM, Jun–Nov

Abingdon Square Greenmarket
Hudson & 12th St.
212-477-3220
Sat, 8AM–Noon, Jun–Dec

City Hall Greenmarket
Center & Chambers St.
212-477-3220
Tue, Fri, 8AM–3PM, year-round

Columbus Circle Greenmarket
8th Ave. & 59th St.
212-477-3220
Thurs, 8AM–5PM, Jul–Dec

Federal Plaza Greenmarket
Federal Building Plaza
Broadway & Thomas St.
212-477-3220
Fri, 8AM–4PM, year-round

**Harlem/New York City Mission
Society Greenmarket**
142nd St. & Lenox Ave.
212-477-3220
Tue, 8AM–3PM, Jul–Nov

Sheffield Plaza Greenmarket
W. 57th & 9th Ave.
212-477-3220
Wed, Sat, 8AM–6PM, year-round

Smith Barney Greenmarket
Greenwich & N. Moore St.
212-477-3220
Wed, 8AM–3PM, year-round

South Ferry Greenmarket
Whitehall & South St.
212-477-3220
Thurs, 8AM–5PM, Jul–Oct

St. Mark's Church Greenmarket
St. Mark's Church courtyard
10th St. & 2nd Ave.
212-477-3220
Tue, 8AM–6PM, Jun–Dec

Union Square Greenmarket
17th & Broadway
212-477-3220
Mon, Wed, Fri, Sat, 8AM–6PM, year-round

**Washington Market Park
Greenmarket**
Greenwich & Reade St.
212-477-3220
Sat, 8AM–3PM, year-round

West 70th Street Greenmarket
Playground, between Amsterdam
& West End Ave.
212-477-3220
Sat, 8AM–5PM, Jul–Nov

West 77th Street Greenmarket
I.S. 44 schoolyard, at Columbus
Ave.
212-477-3220
Sun, 10AM–5PM, year-round

102nd St. Greenmarket
Park playground
Amsterdam Ave.
212-477-3220
Fri, 8AM–2PM, Jun–Nov

175th St. Greenmarket
W. 175th & Broadway
212-477-3220
Thurs, 8AM–6PM, Jun–Dec

**World Trade Center
Greenmarket**
Church & Marginal St., between
Fulton & Vesey St.
212-477-3220
Tue, 8AM–6PM, Jun–Dec; Thurs,
8AM–6PM, year-round

Municipal parking lot
James & Depot St.
914-343-8075
Sat, 8AM–Noon, Jun–Oct

Newburgh City Marketplace
Newburgh Landing
Water & 4th St.
914-565-4250
Tue, Fri, 10AM–6PM, Jul–Nov

Green Seasons Farmers' Market
Anderson St., between North Ave.
& LeCount Pl.
914-654-2186
Fri, 8AM–4PM, Jul–Nov

Niagara Falls City Market
715 Pine St.
716-285-1663
Mon, Wed, Fri, 7AM–5PM, year-round

NORTH SYRACUSE
Trolley Barn Farmers' Market
Chestnut & Bay St.
315-458-8050
Wed, 9AM–7PM, May–Oct

NORTH TONAWANDA
City Market
Robinson & Bryant St.
716-695-8540
Tue, Thurs, Sat, 7AM–1PM, year-round

NORWICH
Chenango County Farmers' Market
East Side Park
Rte. 12 (center of town)
607-334-8310
Mon, Wed, Sat, 8AM–12:30PM, May–Oct

ONEIDA
City of Oneida Farmers' Market
Oneida St. & East end (south side)
315-363-4300
Fri, 8AM–2PM, Jul–Oct

OSSINING
Parking lot at Main & Spring St.
914-762-8515
Sat, 8:30AM–2:30PM, Jun–Nov

OSWEGO
W. 1st St., between Bridge & W. Oneida St.
315-342-1666
Thurs, 5PM–9PM, Jun–Oct

PATCHOGUE
Patchogue Community Market
Ocean Ave., 1 block S. of Main St.
516-581-4576
Fri, Noon–6PM, Jun–Nov

PEEKSKILL
Bank St., between Park & Main St.
914-737-3600
Sat, 8AM–2PM, Jun–Oct

PLATTSBURGH
Trinity Park
518-963-7593
Wed, 9AM–3PM, Jul–Oct

PLEASANT VALLEY
James Baird State Park
Pool Area
Taconic Pkwy., Park exit
914-452-1489
Sun, 1–5PM, Jun–Oct

Town Hall parking lot
Rte. 44
914-635-5038
Fri, 3PM–7PM, Jun–Oct

PORT JEFFERSON
NW corner Main & E. Broadway
516-581-4576
Thurs, Noon–6PM, Jun–Nov

PORT JERVIS
Parking lot, Ball & Front St.
914-856-6694
Sat, 8AM–2PM, Jul–Oct

POTSDAM
Potsdam Farmers' Market
Co-op Store
315-328-4586
Wed, Sat, 9AM–4PM, Jul–Oct

Potsdam Open Farmers' Market
Market St. lot
315-265-4686
Fri, Sat, 8AM–5PM, Jun–Oct

POUGHKEEPSIE
Main Mall, Downtown
914-471-9424
Fri, 8AM–Sellout, Jun–Nov

QUEENS
Flushing Greenmarket
39th Ave. & 39th St.
212-477-3220

RENSSELAER
Ambulance Corps lot
901 3rd St.
518-677-3474
Mon, 3PM–6PM, Jun–Oct

Riverfront Park Farmers' Market
Riverfront Park & Broadway
518-439-4363
Fri, 11AM–2PM, Jun–Oct

RHINEBECK
Rhinebeck Village Municipal parking lot
914-874-4778
Sun, 10AM–2PM, Jun–Oct

ROCHESTER
Downtown Riverwalk Farmers' Market
Bragdon Place, behind Holiday Inn
716-428-6907
Fri, 10AM–2PM, May–Oct

Foodlink Farmers' Market
56 W. Ave.
716-328-3380, ext. 17
Wed, 10AM–2PM, Jul–Oct

Rochester Public Market
280 N. Union St.
716-428-6907
Tue, Thurs, 5AM–Noon, Sat,
5AM–2PM, year-round

West Side Farmers' Market
Lyell Ave., parking lot between
Dewey & Broad
716-889-9251
Fri, 9AM–2PM, Sat, 7AM–2PM,
Jun–Oct

Village Park
Rte. 22 & Main St.
518-854-3750
Sat, 9AM–1PM, Jun–Oct

Spring St. parking lot
518-677-3474
Wed, 3PM–6PM, Sat, 9AM–1PM
May–Oct

Downtown Schenectady Farmers'
Market
Jay & State St.
518-382-5061
Tue, Thurs, 10AM–2PM, May–Oct

George's IGA parking lot
75 N. Ferry Rd.
516-749-0382
Fri, 1PM–Sunset, May–Nov

St. George Greenmarket
Borough Hall
212-477-3220
Sat, 8AM–5PM, Jul–Nov

**Central New York Regional
Market**
2100 Park St.
I-81, exit 23
315-422-8647
Thurs, 11AM–7PM, May–Oct; Sat,
7AM–2PM, year-round

**Downtown Syracuse Farmers'
Market**
Parking lot, S. Salina & W.
Washington St.
315-422-8284
Tue, 7AM–5PM, Jun–Oct

**Downtown Syracuse Winter
Farmers' Market**
City Hall
315-422-8284
Tue, 7AM–5PM, Nov–Jun

Uncle Sam Atrium
Broadway, between 3rd & 4th St.
518-677-3474
Wed, 10AM–2PM, Sat, 9AM–1PM,
May–Oct

Kennedy Parking Garage,
next to City Hall
315-841-3370
Wed, 8AM–5PM, Jun–Oct

**Watertown Farm & Crafts
Market**
Dulles State Office Bldg.
Washington St.
315-785-8286
Wed, 6:30AM–3PM, May–Oct

**Downtown White Plains
Farmers' Market**
Municipal parking lot
Main & Hamilton Ave.
914-422-1336
Wed, 8AM–4PM, Jun–Nov

St. John's Courtyard
Getty Park
914-963-3033
Thurs, 9AM–4PM, Jul–Nov

NORTH CAROLINA

**Biltmore Avenue Tailgate
Market**
Biltmore Ave.
704-658-2922

Tailgaters' Association
Merriman Ave.
704-683-9791

**Western North Carolina
Farmers' Market**
I-40, exit 47
704-253-1691
Year-round

Cedar Falls Park
919-742-5887

**Charlotte Regional Farmers'
Market**
1715 Yorkmont Rd.
704-357-1269
Year-round

2694 Chapel Hill Blvd.
919-489-3944

Greensboro Curb Market
501 Yanceyville St.
919-674-3061
Year-round

Guilford County Food Fair
1810 Phillips Ave.
919-274-5467

Guilford Farmers' Market
3200 Battleground Rd.
919-685-4478
Sat

Guilford Farmers' Market
1416 W. Northwood St.
919-685-4478
Wed

Pitt County Farmers' Market
County Home Road
919-757-2801

Henderson County Curb Market
221 N. Church St.
704-692-8012

Burke Farmers' Market
College St.
704-584-2041

Craven County Farmers' Market
421 Tryon Palace Dr.
919-637-9118
Year-round

New Bern Curb Market
George St.
919-636-4014
Year-round

State Farmers' Market
I-40 (exit 297) & Wheeler Rd.
919-733-7417
Year-round

Wilmington City Market
120-124 S. Front St.
919-343-0042

Forsyth Area Farmers' Fair
Cloverdale Ave.
919-764-1093

Winston-Salem Retail Farmers' Market
Dixie Classic Fairgrounds
919-727-2236

NORTH DAKOTA

Bismarck Farmers' Market
Interstate Ave.
701-224-9973

Community Farmers' Market
Dike East Park
701-347-4933
Tue, Thurs, Sat, 10AM–6:30PM,
Jun–Oct

Greater Grand Forks Farmers' Market
S. Forks Plaza parking lot
701-594-5022

1500 4th Ave. NW
701-838-0012

OHIO

E. State St.
614-593-8555

Court St. Marketplace
513-352-6391

Findlay Market
Elder St.
515-352-6391
Year-round

Tailgate Market
Seymour parking lot
Langdon Farm Rd.
513-352-6391

Pearl Alley Farmers' Market
Pearl Alley
614-752-9816

4th & Market St.
614-264-2212

OKLAHOMA

ADA

12th & Rennie St.
405-332-0702

ARDMORE

Ardmore Main Street Produce Market
107 E. Main
405-226-6246

BROKEN BOW

3rd & Main
405-584-3393

ENID

Garfield County Fairgrounds
405-237-1228

LAWTON

1130 E. Gore Blvd.
405-355-1176, 355-2387
Lawton-Ft. Sill Farmers' Market
Central Mall parking lot
405-355-1176

MUSKOGEE

1440 S. Cherokee
918-687-2458

NORMAN

615 E. Robinson
405-321-4774

OKLAHOMA CITY

Farmers' Public Market
311 Klein St.
405-232-6506

Penn Square Mall, ground floor
405-350-1691, 721-6440

PONCA CITY

100 N. 3rd St.
405-763-8082

SHAWNEE

Pottawatomie County Farmers' Market
Downtown
405-273-7683

STILLWATER

Main Street Farmers' Market
Main St., between 9th & Lewis St.
405-624-2921

TAHLEQUAH

Old Cherokee County Capitol Building
108 S. Mockingbird Lane
918-456-1615

OREGON

ALBANY

Broadalbin & Water St.
503-847-5641
Sat, 8AM–Noon, May–Nov

ALOHA

Aloha Weekend Garden Market
Tri-Met Park & Ride
Cornell Rd. & Bethany, at Hwy. 26
503-359-1705
Sat, 9AM–3PM, May–Oct

ASHLAND

Rogue Valley Growers' & Crafters' Market
Water St., under the Lithia St./Siskyou Blvd. overpass
503-855-1326
Tue, 8:30AM–1:30PM, year-round

ASTORIA

20th & Marine Dr., on the riverfront
503-325-3017
Sat, 9AM–2PM, May–Oct

BEAVERTON

5th & Hall Blvd., behind the Fire Station
503-643-5354
Sat, 8AM–1:30PM, Jun–Oct

CORVALLIS

Benton County Fairgrounds
110 SW 53rd St.
503-847-5641
Wed, 8AM–1PM, May–Nov

Riverfront Park "Green Lot"
1st St., between Madison & Monroe
503-752-1510
Sat, 9AM–1PM, May–Oct

COTTAGE GROVE

Community Center
401½ S. Main St.
503-942-4472
Wed, 3PM–6PM, Jun–Oct

EUGENE

Lane County Farmers' Market
Downtown Mall
Broadway at Willamette
503-342-5856
Wed, 11AM–5:30PM, Jun–Oct
Lane County Farmers' Market
E. 8th & Oak St.
503-342-5856
Sat, 9AM–5PM, Apr–Nov

GRANTS PASS

Grants Pass Growers' Market
4th & F
503-476-5375
Sat, 9AM–1PM, Mar–Nov; Tue,
9AM–1PM, Jun–Sep

GRESHAM

Gresham City Hall parking lot
1333 NW Eastman Pkwy.
503-669-2492
Sat, 8AM–2PM, May–Oct

HILLSBORO

Courthouse Square
503-357-3518
Sat, 8AM–1PM, May–Oct

HOOD RIVER

Jackson Park
13th & May St.
503-386-8766
Sat, 9AM–2PM, Jun–Oct

KLAMATH FALLS

8th St., off Grand
503-882-3888
Sat, 10AM–2PM, Aug–Sep

LA GRANDE

**Blue Mountains Producers
Co-op**
Sunflower Book Store lawn
1114 Washington Ave.
503-963-8049
Sat, 9AM–1:30PM, Jun–Oct

McMINNVILLE

W. Valley Farmers' parking lot
274 N. 99W
503-472-6154
Sat, 9AM–Sellout, Aug–Sep

MEDFORD

**Rogue Valley Growers' and
Crafters' Market**
Medford Center parking lot, out-
side Sears
Jackson St. & Biddle Rd.
503-855-1326
Thurs, 8:30AM–1:30PM, Apr–Nov

NEWPORT

**Lincoln County Small Farmers'
Market**
Lincoln County Fairgrounds
503-444-2059
Sat, 10AM–Noon, May–Oct

PORTLAND

**People's All-Organic Farmers'
Market**
3029 SE 21st St.
503-232-7116, 232-9051
1st Sun of each month, 10AM–2PM,
May–Oct

Portland Farmers' Market
Albers Mill parking lot, on the
Willamette River
1200 NW Front Ave.
503-295-0875
Sat, 8AM–1PM, May–Oct

ROSEBURG

**Douglas County Saturday
Market**
Gove's Market parking lot
Diamond Lake Blvd.
503-459-9485
Sat, 9AM–2PM, Jun–Oct

SALEM

Salem Public Market
1240 Rural St. SE
503-393-3758
Year-round

TIGARD

Magno-Humphries parking lot
Commercial & Hall St.
503-639-1656
Sat, 8AM–1:30PM, Jun–Oct

PENNSYLVANIA

ALLENTOWN

Fairgrounds Market
17th & Chew St.
Thurs, 10AM–8PM, Fri, 8AM–8PM,
Sat, 8AM–6PM, year-round

Lehigh Growers' Market
South Mall
Lehigh St.
610-965-4009
Sat, 9AM–2PM, Jul–Oct

**Turnpike Service Plaza
Farmers' Market**
PA Turnpike, NE Extension (Rte.
9), exit 33 at Rte. 78
717-787-5086
Fri, 11AM–8PM, Sat, 8AM–4PM, Sun,
11AM–7PM, May–Nov

ALTOONA

6th Ave. parking lot
814-224-4844
Thurs, 9AM–2PM, Jul–Oct

BERWICK

1100 block of Mulberry St.
717-379-3279
Tue, Thurs, Sat, 7AM–Noon,
Jun–Oct

BLOOMSBURG

Market Square
717-784-2522
Tue, Thurs, Sat, 7AM–Noon,
Jun–Oct

BUTLER

Butler County Farmers' Market
Shore St. downtown
Mon, Wed, 3PM–6PM, Sat,
7AM–Noon, May–Nov

CARLISLE

260 York Rd.
717-243-5222
Fri, 7AM–5PM, Sat, 7AM–Noon, year-round

CARRICK

City Parks Farmers' Market
Carrick Shopping Center
Brownsville Rd.
412-443-3558
Wed, 4PM–8PM, May–Nov

CLARION

Clarion County Farmers' Market
Clarion Memorial Park
5th & Main
814-764-3790
Sat, 8:30AM–Noon, Jun–Oct

DOYLESTOWN

The Farm Market at Delaware Valley College
Rte. 202 & New Britain Rd.
215-345-1500

State & Hamilton St.
Sat, 6AM–Noon, Apr–Nov

EASTON

Centre Square
Tue, Thurs, Sat, 8am–2pm,
Apr–Dec

EPHRATA

Green Dragon Farmers' Market
Rd. 4 & State St.
717-738-1117
Fri, 8:30AM–9:30PM, Mar–Dec

ERIE

6th & State St.
814-870-1253
Tue, Wed, Thurs, 8AM–4PM,
May–Oct

West Erie Plaza Farmers' Market
4300 W. 12th St.
Wed, Sat, 8AM–5PM, May–Nov

GETTYSBURG

Lincoln Square
717-359-9474
Sat, 7AM–Noon, Jun–Oct

HARRISBURG

Broad St. Market
1233 N. 3rd St.
717-236-7923
Fri, 7AM–5PM, Sat, 7AM–4PM, year-round

Pennsylvania Open Air Farmers' Market
Richard F. Willits Farm Show parking lot
717-761-0939
Tue, Fri, Noon–8PM, May–Nov

HUSTONTOWN

Sideling Hill Turnpike Service Plaza Farmers' Market
Sideling Hill Service Plaza
PA Turnpike (Rte. 76), between
exits 12 & 13
717-787-5086
Fri, 11AM–5PM, Sat, 8AM–5PM, Sun,
11AM–7PM, May–Nov

LANCASTER

Central Market
W. King & Market St.
717-291-4723
Tue, Fri, 6AM–4:30PM; Sat,
6AM–2PM, year-round

LANSDOWNE

Lancaster County Farmers' Market
2 W. Baltimore Pike
610-284-6026
Thurs, Fri, 8AM–7PM, Sat, 8AM–4PM,
year-round

LEESPORT

Leesport Farmers' Market
1 block east. off Rte. 61
610-926-1307
Wed, 9AM–8PM, year-round

LEWISBURG

Fairground Rd.
814-237-1960
Wed, 8AM–7PM, year-round

Flea Market
Rte. 15
Sun, 7AM–5PM, May–Oct

McDONALD

Allegheny Fruit & Vegetable Growers' Association
2152 Old Oakdale Rd.
412-221-7197
Mon, Tue, Wed, 5:30PM–9:30PM, May–Nov

MT. LEBANON

Mt. Lebanon Farmers' Market
733 Washington Rd.
412-344-7623
Wed, 4PM–Dusk, Jun–Oct

McKEESPORT

Lyle Blvd.
412-339-1709
1PM–4:30PM, Jul–Oct

MIDDLETOWN

Saturday's Market
3751 E. Harrisburg Pike
Sat, 7AM–4PM, year-round

PERKASIE

7th & Market St.
215-538-7643
Sat, 7:30AM–Noon, Jun–Oct

PHILADELPHIA

Dutch Country Farmers' Market
2031 Cottman Ave.
215-745-6008
Wed, 9AM–3PM, Thurs, Fri, 8AM–5:30PM, Sat, 8AM–5PM, year-round

Garden Court Farmers' Market
49th & Spruce St.
Sat, 9AM–2PM, May–Dec

Germantown Farmers' Market
5942 Germantown Ave.
215-843-9564
Tue, Fri, 6AM–5PM, year-round

Reading Terminal Market
51 N. 12th & Arch St.
215-922-2317
Mon–Sat, 8AM–6PM, year-round

PITTSBURGH

City Parks Farmers' Market
Allegheny Commons (Northside)
412-443-3558
Fri, 4PM–8PM, May–Nov

City Parks Farmers' Market
Highland Park Zoo parking lot
412-443-3558
Mon, Thurs, 4PM–8PM, May–Nov

County Courthouse Farmers' Market
County Courthouse Building
Fri, 11AM–2PM, May–Nov

Farmers' Co-op Market of East Liberty
Rodman & Sheridan Ave.
412-661-4414
Sat, 5AM–1PM, year-round

Southside Farmers' Market
Municipal parking lot
18th & Sydney
Tue, 4PM–8PM, May–Nov

PITTSTON

Tomato Festival Farmers' Market
City Hall
717-654-0513
Tue, 10AM–4PM, Jul–Nov

POTTSTOWN

300 High St.
Thurs, 8AM–4PM; Fri, 6AM–6PM, Sat, 6AM–2PM, year-round

PUNXSUTAWNEY

Kittanning Farmers' Market
Franklin Village Mall parking lot
Mon–Sat, 8:30AM–Noon, Apr–Dec

QUAKERTOWN

Downtown parking lot
Broad St.
Sat, 8AM–Noon, Jul–Nov

QUARRYVILLE

Quarryville Growers' Market
Good's Store parking lot
610-869-2791
Sat, 9AM–1PM, May–Oct

READING

Reading Fairgrounds Farmers' Market
5th St & Hwy. 222N
Thurs, Fri, 8AM–8PM, Sat, 8AM–4PM, year-round

Reading Farmers' Market
8th & Penn St.
Thurs, Fri, 6AM–5PM, Sat, 6AM–Noon, year-round

SCRANTON

Co-op Farmers' Night Market
900 Barring Ave.
717-563-2258
Mon, Wed, Fri, Noon–7PM, Jul–Nov

SHARON

Downtown Farmers' Market
Parking lot by Reyer's Shoe Store
412-646-2184
Daily, 7AM–Noon, Jul–Nov

One W. State St.
City Center parking lot
412-981-5882
Wed, Sat, 7AM–Noon, Jul–Oct

SHARON HILL

1220-1224 Chester Pike
610-583-7900
Wed, Sat, 6AM–3PM, year-round

STATE COLLEGE

Downtown
Locust Lane,
Fri, 11:30AM–5:30PM, Jun–Nov

TITUSVILLE

Fisher Big Wheel parking lot
110 S. Martin St.
Fri, 10AM–2PM, Jun–Nov

WASHINGTON

Franklin Mall
Hills parking lot
412-663-7344
Mon, Wed, Fri, 5:30PM–Dark; Sat,
Sun, Noon–5PM, Jul–Oct

WEST CHESTER

West Chester Growers' Market
Chestnut & Church St.
610-869-2791
Sat, 9AM–1PM, Jul–Oct

WEST HAZELTON

Hazelton Open Air Market
Churchill Mall
Broad St.
717-379-3286
Tue, Fri, 9AM–3PM, Jun–Oct

WILKES BARRE

Farmers' Night Market
Narrows Shopping Center
Northampton St.
Fri, 4PM–Dusk, Jul–Nov

Public Market
Downtown
717-821-1160
Thurs, 10:45AM–5PM, Jun–Nov

WILLIAMSPORT

**Williamsport Growers'
Association**
Bowman's Field
W. 4th St.
717-745-3395
Fri, Noon–5PM, Jul–Oct

**Williamsport Growers'
Association**
Pine Street Mall
717-745-3395
Tue, 10AM–3PM, Jul–Oct

**Williamsport Growers'
Association**
United Methodist Church parking
lot
Memorial Park & Pine St.
717-745-3395
Sat, 7AM–1PM, Jul–Oct

YORK

Central Market House
34 W. Philadelphia & Beaver St.
717-848-7347
Tue, Thurs, Sat, 6AM–3PM, year-round

**Market & Penn Farmers'
Market**
374 W. Market St.
717-848-1402
Tue, Fri, Sat, 6AM–3PM, year-round

RHODE ISLAND

BLOCK ISLAND

Manisses Corner
401-466-2834

KINGSTON

S. Kingstown Farmers' Market
Kearney Gym
U. of Rhode Island
401-783-0224

PROVIDENCE

Down City Farmers' Market
Kennedy Plaza
401-273-9419

**Governor Dyer Cooperative
Market**
Between Promenade, Valley,
Rathbone & Hemlock St.
401-273-8800

WESTERLY

Downtown Farmers' Market
High St.
401-348-1253

SOUTH CAROLINA

COLUMBIA

**Columbia State Farmers'
Market**
Columbia Market
803-253-4041
Daily, 6AM–9PM, year-round

FLORENCE

Pee Dee Farmers' Market
Hwy. 52
803-665-5154
Year-round

GREENVILLE

1354 Rutherford Rd.
803-244-1023
Year-round
West End Market
13 Augusta St.
803-467-4412

JEFFERSON

Hwy. 151
803-658-3251

SOUTH DAKOTA

BELLE FOURCHE

415 5th Ave.
605-773-5436

PIERRE

**Chamber of Commerce
Farmers' Market**
108 E. Missouri Ave.
605-773-5436

RAPID CITY

Black Hills Farmers' Market
1015 Kansas St.
605-348-7165

SIOUX FALLS

Downtown Farmers' Market
415 S. 1st Ave.
605-773-5436

VERMILLION

1870 Constance Dr.
605-773-5436

TENNESSEE

CHATTANOOGA
11th St. Farmers' Market
734 E. 12th St.
615-267-4492
Year-round

JOHNSON CITY
Tri-Cities F.A.R.M.
St. John Episcopal Church
615-323-9641

KNOXVILLE
East Tennessee F.A.R.M.
Hendrons Chapel
Rte. 9
615-575-6409
**Knox County Regional
Farmers' Market**
4700 New Harvest Ln.
615-521-2275
Year-round

Western Ave. Market
124 Dale Ave.
615-522-7157

MEMPHIS

Agricenter
7777 Walnut Grove Rd.
901-756-4247
Scott St. Market
814 Scott St.
901-327-8828

MURFREESBORO
**Ritherford County Farmers'
Market**
South Front St.
615-893-9177

NASHVILLE
Metro Farmers' Market
618 Jackson St.
615-259-7903
Year-round
Nashville F.A.R.M.
(5 locations)
615-298-4760

OAK RIDGE
East Tennessee F.A.R.M.
107 Dartmouth
615-483-0751

SHELBYVILLE
**Bedford County Farmers'
Market**
County Celebration Grounds
615-648-5971

SPARTA
White County Farmers' Market
County Fairgrounds
615-836-3348

TEXAS

ABILENE

Taylor County Fairgrounds
915-548-2751
Wed, Sat, Sun, 8AM–Sellout

AMARILLO
**Golden Spread Farmers'
Market**
1000 W. 8th & Washington St.
806-352-7078
Tue, Thurs, Sat, 7:30AM–Sellout

AUSTIN

6701 Burnet Rd.
512-454-1002
Mon-Sat, 8AM–6PM, Sun, AM–4PM
Year-round

Austin South Farmers' Market
Pickle Rd., off S. Congress Ave.
512-285-4758
Sat, 8AM–Sellout, year-round

E. 7th & Martinez St.
Wed, Sun, 3–6PM

209656 Helena St.
409-794-2532
Tue, Thurs, Sat, 6AM–Sellout, year-round

Comfort Community Park, (off Hwy. 27)
512-995-3884
Wed, 8AM–Sellout

120 Water St.
512-882-9209
Tue, Thurs, Sat, 7AM–3PM

San Felipe's Lion Park
512-757-1495
Mon, Wed, Fri, 8AM–Sellout

Kmart parking lot
University & Bonni Area
817-365-2201
Tue, Thurs, Sat, 8AM–5PM

Ave. of the Americas & Isleta Rd.
915-592-7130
Sat, Sun, 7AM–5PM

Border Tobacco parking lot
501 E. Paisano Rd.
915-592-7130
Tue, 7AM–Sellout

Kmart
6375 Montana Ave.
915-592-7130
Sat, 7AM–Sellout

Kmart
411 N. Zaragosa Rd.
915-592-7130
Wed, 6:30AM–12:30PM

Sunrise Shopping Center
8500 Dyer
915-592-7130
Sun, 7AM–Sellout

Polytechnical Heights
1516 Vaughn
817-644-5523
Tue, Fri, 8AM–6:30PM, year-round

207 E. Park St
512-997-5008
Wed, Sat, 8AM–Sellout, year-round

2525 Airline Dr.
Mon–Sat, 2:30PM–5PM, Sun, 2:30PM–6PM, year-round

Westwood Mall Freeway
Bissonnett & SW, off Hwy. 59
Sat, 8AM–Noon

4th & Gray St.
Tue, Fri, 3PM–6PM

S. University, at 12th St.
806-828-3454
Tue, Thurs, Sat, 8AM–Sellout

Angelina County Farmers' Market
2107 S. Medford
409-634-6655
Daily, 7AM–Sellout

1505 E. Front
915-694-0571
Mon, Fri, 8AM–Sellout
Permian Basin Farmers' Market
5021 Princeton
915-694-0571
Thurs, Sat, 8AM–Sellout

Comal County Fairgrounds
512-629-6434
Fri, 5PM–Sellout

4703 Golder
915-694-0571
Tue, Thurs, Sat, 8AM–Sellout

Market Square
214-785-3502
Mon–Sat, 7AM–Dusk

I-27 & Hwy. 70W, across from WalMart
806-684-2439
Wed, Sat, 8AM–Sellout

PORT ARTHUR

Jefferson County Farmers' Market
1910 Woodworth
409-983-5300
Tue, Thurs, Fri, 7AM–6PM

ROBSTOWN

Nueces County Farmers' Market
Nueces County Showbarn
Hwy. 77 & Hwy. 44
512-387-5904
Fri, Noon–Sellout, year-round

SAN ANGELO

1005 Fairview Dr.
915-653-7348
Tue, Thurs, 5PM–Sellout, Sat,
8AM–Sellout

SAN ANTONIO

Hamilston Wolfe & Babcock Rd.
512-922-8472
Year-round

Leon Valley Community Center
Evers Rd.
512-922-8472
Wed, 8AM–Sellout, year-round

Olmos Basin Park
Jackson-Keller Rd.
512-922-8472
Sat, 8AM–Sellout

2823 Hillcrest
512-922-8472
Year-round

TEMPLE

Belton County Farmers' Market
Municipal Building
200 E. Central
817-770-5605
Tue, Thurs, 7:30AM–Sellout, year-round

TEXARKANA

3920 Summerhill Rd.
903-667-3164
Tue, Thurs, Sat, 7AM–Sellout

TYLER

East Texas Fairgrounds
214-535-0885
Tue, Thurs, Sat, 7AM–Sellout

WACO

Heart of Texas Fairgrounds
4601 Bosque Blvd.
817-799-8659
Tue, Thurs, Sat, 8AM–Sellout, year-round

WICHITA FALLS

8th & Ohio St.
817-761-8820
Mon–Sat, 7:30AM–5:30PM, year-round

UTAH

MURRAY

Utah Farm Bureau Farmers' Market
5300 S. 360 West
801-261-4864

SALT LAKE CITY

Downtown Alliance Farmers' Market
Pioneer Park
801-359-5118

SPANISH FORK

City Park
Center & Main St.
801-798-5000

VERMONT

BENNINGTON

Chamber of Commerce grounds
Veteran's Memorial Dr.
802-375-9403
Wed, Fri, 10AM–4PM, Jun–Oct

BRATTLEBORO

Rte. 9, just west of covered bridge,
behind Mobil station at West
Brattleboro
802-254-9567
Sat, 9AM–2PM, May–Oct

Town Common
802-254-9567
Wed, 10AM–2PM, Jun–Sep

BURLINGTON

City Hall Park
College St.
802-865-9803
Sat, 9AM–2:30PM, May–Oct

Old North End Neighborhood Farmers' Market
H. O. Wheeler School
Archibald St.
802-863-6248
Tue, 3:30–6:30PM, Jun–Oct

LONDONDERRY

West River Farmers' Market
Mill Tavern
Rte. 11 & Rte. 100
802-824-4486
Sat, 9AM–1PM, May–Oct

MIDDLEBURY

Middlebury Union High School
802-897-5971
Wed, 9AM–Noon, Jun–Aug; Sat,
9AM–Noon, Jun–Oct

MONTPELIER

Capital City Farmers' Market
Courthouse parking lot
802-479-9701
Sat, 9AM–1PM, May–Oct

RUTLAND

Rte. 7S, behind Kinney Motors
802-446-2018
Sat, 8AM–2PM, May–Oct; Wed,
8AM–2PM, Jun–Sep

ST. JOHNSBURY

Caledonia Farmers' Market
Middle School
Western Ave.
802-748-9902
Wed, 9AM–1PM, Jun–Aug; Sat,
9AM–1PM, Jun–Oct

SOUTH WOODSTOCK

Mount Tom Farmers' Market
Rte. 12N
802-457-1520
Sat, 9AM–1PM, May–Oct

STOWE

Mountain Rd., next to Red Barn
Shops
802-253-4498
Sun, 11AM–3PM, May–Oct

WAITSFIELD

**Mad River Green Farmers'
Market**
Rte. 100
802-496-5856
Sat, 9:30AM–1:30PM, May–Oct

WATERBURY

Rusty Parker Park
902-244-8454
Wed, 3PM–6PM, May–Oct

VIRGINIA

APPOMATOX

Main St.
804-352-2621

ARLINGTON

Arlington County Farmers' Market
N. 14th & N. Courthouse
703-358-6400

CHARLOTTESVILLE

City Farmers' Market
Carver Recreation Center
804-971-3271

CULPEPER

Clintwood Farmers' Market
Main St.
703-926-4605

East Davis & Connors St.
703-948-3310

FAIRFAX

**Fairfax Extension Farmers'
Market**
Truro Lane
703-324-5390

FREDERICKSBURG

Prince Edward St.
703-372-1010

HARRISONBURG

Water St.
703-269-8261

HERNDON

Spring St., next to Town Mall
703-324-5390

LYNCHBURG

Community Farmers' Market
Main & 12th St.
804-847-1499

MANASSAS

City Farmers' Market
Center & West St. (gazebo area)
703-361-6599

McLEAN

1659 Chain Bridge Rd.
703-327-5390

MT. VERNON

2511 Parkers Ln.
703-324-5390

NEWPORT NEWS

Patrick Henry Farmers' Market
Patrick Henry Mall
804-596-2111

RICHMOND

Richmond Farmers' Market
17th & Main St.
804-780-8597

ROANOKE

Historic City Farmers' Market
Market Square
Campbell St.
703-982-3504
Year-round

VIENNA

Nottoway Park
703-324-5390

VIRGINIA BEACH

1989 Landstown Ave.
804-427-4395
Year-round

WILLIAMSBURG

James City County Farmers' Market
3617 Strawberry Plain Rd.
804-229-2625

WASHINGTON

COLVILLE

Northeast Washington Farmers' Market
Main St. & Tiger Hwy.
509-738-2547

KENT

Kent Saturday Market
2nd & Smith
206-859-3369
Sat

LONGVIEW

Cowlitz Community Farmers' Market
5th & Washington
206-425-4835

MT. VERNON

Skagit Valley Farmers' Market
Downtown, under tulip smoke-stack
206-428-8547

OLYMPIA

Capitol Way & Thurston
206-352-9096

PASCO

4th & Lewis
509-545-0738

PORT ANGELES

8th & Chase St.
206-683-7089

PORT TOWNSEND

Water St.
206-732-4675

REDMOND

Redmond Saturday Market
7730 Leary Way
206-488-2405
Sat

SEATTLE

Pike Place Market
1st Ave. & Pike
206-682-7451
Daily, year-round

SPOKANE

Spokane Marketplace
20 E. Riverside
509-482-2627

TACOMA

9th & Broadway St.
206-272-8481

VANCOUVER

502 Main
206-574-5242

WENATCHEE

Wenatchee Valley Farmers' Market
Riverfront Park
509-884-8985

WEST VIRGINIA

CHARLESTON

Downtown, near State
Deptartment. of Agriculture
304-558-0185
Year-round

ELKINS

Street & Railroad Ave.
304-636-2455

MARTINSBURG

Queen & King St.
304-267-4841

MORGANTOWN

High St.
304-291-7201

WISCONSIN

APPLETON

Goodwill parking lot
414-725-4231
Sat, 6AM–Sellout, Apr–Oct

W. Washington & N. Superior
414-954-9112
Sat, 7:30AM–Noon, Jul–Oct

CHIPPEWA FALLS

16 W. Columbia St.
715-723-7858
Mon, Thurs, 3PM–7PM, Jun–Oct

EAU CLAIRE

Railroad St. parking lot
715-839-0011
Wed, Sat, 7:30AM–1PM, Jun–Oct

London Square Mall
715-285-5351
Wed, Sat, 7:30AM–Sellout, Jun–Oct

FOND DU LAC

**Portland Street Farmers'
Market**
Portland Street
414-921-9500
Sat, 6AM–1PM, Jun–Oct

Main & Forest
414-921-9500
Wed, 8AM–3PM, Jul–Oct

GREEN BAY

Cherry & Quincy
414-448-3300
Sat, 7AM–Noon, Jul–Oct

Military & Mason
414-448-3300
Wed, 7AM–Noon, Jul–Oct

KENOSHA

Roosevelt/Anderson Park
414-635-6434
Mon, 6AM–Noon, Jun–Nov

Union Park
45th St. & 8th Ave.
414-635-6434
Tue, 6AM–Noon, Jun–Nov

Columbus Park
414-635-6434
Wed, 6AM–Noon, Jun–Nov

54th St. & 22nd Ave.
414-635-6434
Sat, 6AM–1PM, Jun–Nov

Lincoln Park
18th Ave. & 70th St.
414-635-6434
Thurs, 6AM–Noon, Jun–Nov

Baker Park
66th St. & Sheridan Rd.
414-635-6434
Fri, 6AM–Noon, Jun–Nov

LA CROSSE

Bridgeview Plaza
800-659-9424
Wed, 8AM–Sellout, Sat,
7AM–Sellout, Jun–Oct

City Hall parking lot
1-800-659-9424
Sat, 6AM–Sellout, Jun–Oct

MADISON

Capitol Square
414-563-5037
Sat, 6AM–2PM, Apr–Nov

Hilldale Shopping Center
608-238-6353
Wed, Sat, 7AM–2PM, May–Oct

Post Office & City County
Building
414-563-5037
Wed, 9AM–2PM, May–Oct

MILWAUKEE

Mitchell St. & 13th
414-223-5817
Mon–Sat, 6AM–6PM, Apr–Oct

4th & Wisconsin Ave.
414-223-5817
Wed, 10AM–4PM, Apr–Oct

2200 Fond du Lac
414-223-5817
Mon–Sat, 6AM–6PM, Apr–Oct

OSHKOSH

Soolin parking lot
Algoma & Division
414-424-7700
Wed, 8AM–Noon, Jun–Oct

Boeder & Stephen parking lot
9th & Oregon
414-424-7700
Sat, 8AM–Noon, Jun–Oct

RACINE

2nd & Main
414-886-3284
Wed, 7AM–4PM, Apr–Nov

West End
21st St., next to Sam's Club
414-886-3284
Tue, Fri, 8AM–1PM, May–Nov

SHEBOYGAN

8th & Niagara
414-457-7272
Wed, Sat, 7AM–3PM, Jun–Nov

STURGEON BAY

Market Square
414-746-2914
Sat, 9AM–Noon, Jun–Oct

WAUKESHA

Main & Barstow
414-549-6154
Tue, Thurs, 6AM–1PM, Jun–Nov

WAUSAU

River Dr.
715-359-4425
Daily, May–Oct; Wed, Sat, 2nd &
3rd week in Nov

WISCONSIN DELLS

Bowman Park
Broadway & Bowman
608-254-7458, 8AM–Sellout,
Jul–Oct

WYOMING

BUFFALO

55 N. Main
307-684-5544

CASPAR

2011 Fairgrounds Rd.
307-235-9400

CHEYENNE

1620 Central Ave.
307-635-9291

CANADA

BRITISH COLUMBIA

ROBERTS CREEK

Organic Market
Community Hall
Sun, 9AM–Noon

VANCOUVER

Granville Island Public Market
1669 Johnson St.
604-666-6477
Mon, Tue, Wed, Thurs, early
AM–Sellout, year-round

WHISTLER

Sun, 9AM–Sellout

NEW BRUNSWICK

FREDERICTON

Boyce Farmers' Market
Sat, 8AM–Sellout

St. John City Market
Mon–Sat, 8AM–Sellout

NOVA SCOTIA

Harvest Line: 1-800-679-6063
Up-to-date hotline for farmers'
markets & fresh produce

HALIFAX

The Brewery
Lower Water St.
Year-round

ONTARIO

Ontario Berry Hotline: 1-800-
263-3262 (operates June 1-July 31)

BURLINGTON

**Burlington Downtown
Farmers' Market**
Off Brant St., across from City Hall
Sat, 8AM–2PM, Jun–Oct

**Burlington Mall Farmers'
Market**
Burlington Mall parking lot
Guelph Line & Fairview St.
Wed, 9AM–5PM, May–Nov

CAMBRIDGE

40 Dickson St.
Wed, 5:45AM–1PM, Jun–Oct; Sat,
5:45AM–1PM, year-round

CORNWALL

**Seaway Valley Growers'
Farmers' Market**
North end of Pitt St. & Cornwall
Centre Rd.
Wed, Sat, 7AM–1PM, Jul–Oct

GUELPH

Gordon St. & Waterloo Ave., at
railway underpass
Thurs, 11AM–6PM, Jun–Nov; Sat,
7AM–Noon, year-round

HAMILTON

Centre Mall Farmers' Market
1227 Barton St. East, between
Ottawa & Kenilworth St.
Wed, 8AM–5:30PM, May–Nov; Fri,
Sat, 8AM–5:30PM, year-round

KINGSTON

Kingston Farmers' Market

KITCHENER

Kitchener Farmers' Market
Duke & Scott St.
519-741-2287

Market Square
Frederick & Duke St.
Sat, 6AM–2PM, year-round

NIAGARA FALLS

Park Street Market
Park St. between Crysler Ave. &
St. Clair
Sat, 6AM–1PM, year-round

Sylvia Place Market
Near corner of Main & Ferry St.
Sat, 6AM–1PM, year-round

NORTH GOWER

North Gower Farmers' Market
613-489-2219
Sat, 6AM–Sellout

OSHAWA

**Oshawa Downtown Farmers'
Market**
Simcoe St. North at Richmond St.
Sat, 8AM–2PM, May–Oct

**Oshawa Centre Farmers'
Market**
Oshawa Shopping Centre
King St. West & Stevenson Rd.
Fri, Dawn–Dusk, May–Oct

OTTAWA

**Byward Farmers' Market
(Downtown)**
Market Square
55 Byward Ave.
Sun, Mon, 6AM–6PM, Apr–Dec

OWEN SOUND

110 8th St. East, beside City Hall
WED, 7A–Noon, JUL–AUG; SA, 7A–
Noon, year-round

PORT COLBORNE

Market Square
Catherine, Charlotte & Clarence St.
Fri, 6AM–1PM, year-round

ST. JACOB'S

St. Jacob's Farmers' Market
519-747-1830

SAULT STE. MARIE

Algoma Farmer' Market
Roberta Bondar Pavillion
Sat, 8AM–12:30PM, May–Jun; Sat,
7AM–12:30PM, Jul–Sep; Sat,
8AM–12:30PM, Oct

SUDBURY

**Downtown Sudbury Festival
Farmers' Market**
Shaunessy St. city carpark, next to
Sudbury Theatre Centre
Sat, Sun, 7AM–5PM, May–Oct

THUNDER BAY

Ft. Williams Curling Club
Ft. Williams Gardens
Tue, Fri, 7:30AM–11:30PM, Jul–Sep

Intercity Shopping Mall
1000 Ft. William Rd.
Isabel St. & Neebing McIntyre
Floodway, Memorial Ave.
Thurs, 6PM–9PM, Jul–Sep; Wed,
1PM–3PM, Sep–Oct

Northwood Park Plaza parking lot
Edward & Redwood St.
Sat, 1PM–4PM, May–Jun; Sat,
1PM–3PM, Aug–Oct

Victoriaville Mall
South Ward
Thurs, F, 8AM–2:30PM, May–Jul;
Tue, Fri, 8AM–2:30PM, Sep–Nov

Wilson Street Park
City Park
Wed, Sat, 8:30AM–11:30AM,
May–Oct

TORONTO

St. Lawrence Farmers' Market
92 Front St. East at Jarvis St.
Thurs, 8AM–6PM, Sat, 5AM–5PM,
year-round

**Toronto Harvest Days Farmers'
Market**
Toronto City Hall
Nathan Phillips Square
Wed, 11AM–3:30PM, Jun–Oct

TRENTON

The Trenton Market
Front St. parking lot
Tue, Thurs, Sat, 6AM–2PM,
Apr–Nov

Trenton Farmers' Market
William St., on the western shore
of the Trent River between the
two Trenton City bridges
Tue, Thurs, Sat, 6AM–2PM,
Mar–Nov

WATERLOO

Waterloo County Farmers' Market
Weber St. North (outside city
limits)
Wed, 8AM–2PM, Jun–Oct; Sat,
6AM–2PM, year-round

WOODSTOCK

Woodstock Fairgrounds
875 Nellis St.
Sat, 7AM–Noon, year-round

MANITOBA

BOISSEVAIN
204-534-6637
Fri, 10AM–Noon

CARBERRY
204-834-3000
Thurs, 9AM–11AM

LAC DU BONNET
204-345-8060
Sat, 10AM–1PM

Mac GREGOR
204-252-2759
Fri, 10AM–1PM

Mc CREARY
204-835-2373
Fri, 9AM–11AM

PILOT MOUND
204-825-2305
Fri, 3PM–5PM

PORTAGE LA PRAIRIE
204-267-2162
Wed, 5PM–8PM; Sat, 9AM–Noon

ST. NORBERT
204-261-3795
Sat, 8AM–2PM

SWAN RIVER
204-734-3417
Thurs, 4:30PM–6:30PM

TEULON
204-886-2618
Sat, 8:30AM–1PM

THE PAS
204-623-3674
Sat, 9AM–Noon

PRINCE EDWARD ISLAND

CHARLOTTETOWN

100 Belvedere Ave.
Tue, Thurs, Sat, 9AM–2PM, Jul–Aug;
Sat, 9AM–2PM, year-round

KENSINGTON

Kensington & Area Farmers' Market
Old Train Station
Broadway St.
Sat, 9AM–3PM, Jul–Oct

WOOD ISLANDS

Wood Islands Farmers' Market Co-op
Rte. 1, opposite ferry compound
Daily, 10AM–6PM, year-round

Recipe Index